Environmental Improvement Through
Economic Incentives

Environmental Improvement Through Economic Incentives

Frederick R. Anderson   Allen V. Kneese

Phillip D. Reed   Russell B. Stevenson

Serge Taylor

Published for

RESOURCES FOR THE FUTURE

by The Johns Hopkins University Press

Baltimore and London

Copyright © 1977 by The Johns Hopkins University Press

All rights reserved

Manufactured in the United States of America

Library of Congress Catalog Card Number 76-47400

ISBN 0-8018-2000-6

ISBN 0-8018-2100-2 paper

Library of Congress Cataloging in Publication Data will be found
on the last printed page of this book.

RESOURCES FOR THE FUTURE, INC.
1755 Massachusetts Avenue, N.W., Washington, D.C. 20036

Resources for the Future is a nonprofit organization for research and education in the development, conservation, and use of natural resources and the improvement of the quality of the environment. It was established in 1952 with the cooperation of the Ford Foundation. Grants for research are accepted from government and private sources only if they meet the conditions of a policy established by the Board of Directors of Resources for the Future. The policy states that RFF shall be solely responsible for the conduct of the research and free to make the research results available to the public. Part of the work of Resources for the Future is carried out by its resident staff; part is supported by grants to universities and other nonprofit organizations. Unless otherwise stated, interpretations and conclusions in RFF publications are those of the authors; the organization takes responsibility for the selection of significant subjects for study, the competence of the researchers, and their freedom of inquiry.

This book was prepared under a grant from RFF's quality of the environment division, directed by Walter O. Spofford, Jr. It was edited by Ruth B. Haas.

RFF editors: Joan R. Tron, Ruth B. Haas, Jo Hinkel, Sally A. Skillings

Contents

Foreword

The use of money charges to discourage environmental harm has long been viewed as a theoretically attractive complement to our existing programs of direct administrative regulation. Very little thought has been given, however, to the practical problems of implementing such strategies. This book, which is a joint project of Resources for the Future and the Environmental Law Institute, attempts to remedy that defect by addressing the economic, technical, legal, and political problems which must be overcome before charges plans can become a working reality.

The authors make a special contribution to policy studies which we are confident will be emulated in the future. Environmental policy research has tended to overlook the complex and deceptive dynamics of implementation, focusing instead on the politics of securing legislative enactment and on the expected impacts of legislative programs which it is simply assumed will function as planned. The authors undertook the present analysis in the belief that legislative goals and program impacts are fundamentally altered by the course which implementation takes. Consequently, they dwell upon a key challenge to effective government which others have neglected. The message for legislators in particular is plain: they must think about *how* to get the job done at the same time they are deciding *what* policies to adopt.

This book, first begun in 1970, has evolved steadily over the years. The first draft of the manuscript was prepared by Frederick Anderson, Laurence Moss, Serge Taylor, and Adrian Wood for the Committee on Public Engineering Policy of the National

Academy of Engineering. The draft enjoyed a mild notoriety in two respects. First, the Committee concluded that while the study had many outstanding merits, the manuscript was different in kind from most Committee publications and suggested that the authors seek an outside publisher. Contrary to suggestions that the Committee "suppressed" the study, however, it was sympathetically received.[1] Second, in 1970 the draft study was used by the Council on Environmental Quality and the White House in developing the Nixon administration's proposals for a sulfur dioxide charge and a horsepower tax. The Council and the White House each apparently relied upon the study in arriving at their "independent" assessments of the other's position.[2]

Under the leadership of Frederick Anderson, a new set of coauthors substantially revised the manuscript before final publication. Between the first and the last drafts, the national political context for charges has improved, the authors have had ample opportunity to resolve their many differences of opinion, and the manuscript has benefited from circulation among a large number of interested policy makers and scholars. The result is an important addition to the growing literature on new environmental management techniques.

April 1977
CRAIG MATHEWS   CHARLES J. HITCH
President   President
Environmental Law Institute   Resources for the Future

---

[1] For example, John F. Burby, "An Unpublished Basic Document," *National Journal* October 21, 1972, p. 1645; Phillip Boffey, *The Brain Bank of America: An Inquiry into the Politics of Science* (New York, McGraw-Hill, 1975) pp. 73–74.

[2] Burby, "An Unpublished Basic Document." (At the time, the draft included a quantitative analysis of the charge level for sulfur oxides which would cause a cutback in emissions to then-approved safe ambient standards.)

Preface

We intend this book for all readers concerned about basic environmental management strategies, but especially for federal and state legislators, committee staff members, agency personnel, political scientists, economists, planners, engineers, and attorneys who are directly involved in developing environmental policies and controls.

Much of what we have written applies to the national scene, and we hope that our work particularly benefits policy makers in the federal government. We believe, however, that some of the best opportunities for implementation of the charges approach exist in the states. While most advocates of charges expected that the first effective charges plans would be federal and would focus on air or water pollution, the states actually have been the first to act, primarily by using charges to curtail the misuse of land and recyclable resources.

Copies of the original draft of this book are still in circulation within several federal and state agencies and the academic community. We feel a bit like manufacturers who have distributed a product that has turned out to be dangerous and now are obliged to provide a replacement. Since we now have the benefit of further research, we caution that reliance upon our earlier analysis could have serious consequences, including to our reputations.

We have focused upon the economic, technical, legal, and political aspects of charges plans, although we realize that we have not nearly exhausted the relevant disciplinary perspectives. Frederick Anderson of the Environmental Law Institute, who had overall

responsibility for the book, wrote chapters 1 and 5. Allen Kneese, professor of economics at the University of New Mexico, authored chapter 2, which covers the theoretical economic underpinnings of environmental charges. It is short because the contributions of economic analysis have been fully explored in earlier publications.[1] Russell Stevenson, associate professor of law at George Washington University (and an engineer), wrote chapter 4 and the first draft of chapter 3. Serge Taylor, assistant professor of political science at the University of Michigan, prepared the political analysis contained in chapter 6. The authors owe a particular debt of gratitude to the latecomer to their circle, Phillip Reed, also an attorney with the Environmental Law Institute, who rewrote chapters 2 and 3 and provided many useful passages for other chapters.

We wish to thank a variety of individuals who over the years have commented upon our draft chapters. We excuse them, however, from sharing with us any blame for errors of fact or analysis which lie in these pages. We are grateful for their helpful comments to Richard Ayres, Blair Bower, Harvey Brooks, David Cavers, Robert Dorfman, William Drayton, Ward Elliott, Myrick Freeman, Kochiro Fujikura, Harvey Garn, Julian Gresser, Helen Ingram, Will Irwin, Jack Knetsch, James Krier, Lee Lane, Charles Meyers, Laurence Moss, Marc Roberts, Susan Rose-Ackerman, Larry Ruff, Peter Sand, Edward Selig, Frederick Smith, Richard Stewart, Robert Anderson, and William J. Vaughan. We are indebted to others too numerous to mention for their suggestions of charges approaches for inclusion in chapter 3.

April 1977   FREDERICK R. ANDERSON
                                                Environmental Law Institute

---

[1] Allen V. Kneese, *The Economics of Regional Water Quality Management* (Baltimore, Johns Hopkins University Press for Resources for the Future, 1964); Allen V. Kneese and Blair T. Bower, *Managing Water Quality: Economics, Technology, Institutions* (Baltimore, Johns Hopkins University Press for Resources for the Future, 1968); Allen V. Kneese and Charles L. Schultze, *Pollution, Prices, and Public Policy* (Washington, Brookings Institution, 1975); Larry Ruff, "The Economic Common Sense of Pollution," *The Public Interest* (Spring, 1970) p. 69, and articles cited in chapter 2.

1

Introduction

This book is about a strategy for environmental control, which, except for some limited minor experiments, has not been seriously tried in the United States. In this strategy, a legislature authorizes a money charge on environmentally harmful conduct; by raising the costs of continuing that conduct, the charge helps persuade the entity causing the harm to adopt less costly, more environmentally acceptable means of achieving its goals. Charges could be used in this way to combat a great variety of environmental problems. Examples include air and water pollutants, the lead content of gasoline, automobile weight or horsepower, congestion on highways and at parking lots and recreational facilities, noise, throwaway containers and other solid wastes, and a variety of undesirable land use practices.

Theoretical economists have advocated the charges concept for many years. In the mid-1960s the pollution control committees in Congress gave the concept a brief, lukewarm review, but rejected it as a principal strategy. A decade later, however, a wide variety of economic incentives have been proposed to achieve energy conservation goals. A handful of programs that incorporate some or all of the elements of the charges approach have actually been implemented in a few states and abroad. The "bottle bills" in four states and some local jurisdictions, the civil penalty provision in Connecticut's environmental control law, and the Vermont land gains tax are promising experiments. Western Germany, Hungary, France, and the Netherlands have developed versions of effluent charges, with varying degrees of success. Japan and Singapore,

Malaysia, are experimenting with charges to reduce congestion. There are many other additional proposals for the use of charges. Chapter 3 will provide a closer look at some functioning and proposed charges systems and related approaches.

This book is an attempt to examine the economic, legal, engineering, and political aspects of charges. It begins with a brief overview of the theoretical rationale which economists have already supplied. It then moves on to consider engineering feasibility (primarily monitoring), legal foundations and pitfalls, and the political factors affecting the enactment of charges programs. Like many legislative proposals, complex economic, engineering, legal, and political elements must be considered as a whole before a viable charge program can be designed.[1]

Adoption of the charges approach would require a rethinking of many of the basic premises upon which environmental controls have been based to date. The method that the United States has used to carry out its most important and advanced programs has almost invariably been direct regulation. This is true nationally for control of air and water pollution, pesticides, noise, and radiation, for example, and locally for land use and, to some extent, solid waste disposal. Under the direct regulatory approach, the appropriate level of government sets standards of behavior or maximum allowable amounts of discharge for particular pollutants and industries, and administrative and judicial means are used to enforce these standards. This approach has yielded important gains in the struggle against environmental harm. The growth of environmental pollutants and environmentally harmful activities has been slowed and in some instances actually reversed.

Yet, more and more questions are being raised about the regulatory programs which are currently in force. They are costly and cumbersome, and contain defects that chronically forestall a significant reduction in environmental harm. If these programs can-

[1] See also William A. Irwin and Richard A. Liroff, *Economic Disincentives for Pollution Control: Legal, Political and Administrative Dimensions* (Washington, GPO, 1974). This study by two colleagues at the Environmental Law Institute carefully defines disincentives; distinguishes them from other similar social policy implements such as fines, user charges and license fees; discusses the constitutionality of disincentives; surveys some disincentive approaches; and particularly explores the legal and administrative dimensions of use of disincentives within the existing statutory mandates of the Environmental Protection Agency.

not show more impressive gains at a reasonable price within the next few years, many persons fear that legislatures will weaken them or cast them aside in discouragement. More effective, efficient alternatives must be made available to legislatures so that the quest for environmental improvement does not falter if existing programs prove inadequate. We address in this book what we believe to be the most promising new approach.

As indicated, the basic concept behind charges is fairly easy to understand: the obligation to pay when environmental harm is produced provides an incentive not to cause that harm. But when properly implemented, charges have additional features which, if they are to be fully appreciated, require some explanation of how the environment and the economy are related. Thus several basic economic concepts are discussed first. The essentials can be simply conveyed in this brief introduction; chapter 2 discusses them more fully.

Prices and the Environment

The concepts which must be understood before the connection between environmental problems and the economy is clear are the role of prices in allocating resources, the damaging environmental consequences of the free use of valuable resources that as yet have no prices, and the manner in which these resources can be given prices. In a market economy, which the United States still enjoys in a modified form, prices perform the key function of allocating all types of resources—raw materials, production capacity, goods, services—to their most efficient use. When the markets in the economy are functioning properly, the price each resource can command is equal to the value of other resources that are used in producing it. In an economically efficient market, it is not possible to produce an additional unit of a good without reducing the production of another good. One individual cannot be given more of any good without someone else getting less.

However, many environmental resources are still unpriced and remain outside the market. Because ownership rights have not been assigned to them, and because they are not easily broken up into units that can be bought and sold, such valuable environ-

mental assets as watercourses, the air mantle, landscape features, and even silence are "used up," but their use is not accurately reflected in the price system. Economists describe the harms caused by such use as "externalities," because the burden of the resources consumed falls on society at large, not just on the user who actually consumes them.

Usually such resources are consumed on a first-come, first-served basis—industrial air pollution spoils clear, breathable air; upstream polluters preclude downstream uses; noisy transportation and construction crowd out silence; and discarded beverage containers litter a community's open spaces. It is true that joint, non-exclusive uses may sometimes be possible. But such common property resources as clean air, open spaces, and even sunlight are increasingly scarce because of preemptive uses that do not take into account the fairness and overall social desirability of the choices made.

The result may be a free-for-all contest for limited resources. The end result of such a contest was pointed out by Garrett Hardin in 1968. Citing a scenario first sketched as a mathematical exercise in 1833 by William Forster Lloyd, Hardin describes a pasture that is open to all, in which each herdsman tries to graze as many cattle as possible. Because the herdsman obtains all the positive benefits from grazing the cattle, and because the negative effects of overgrazing are spread among all users of the commons, it is economically rational for him to behave in this way. Since each herdsman is still adding to his herd as much as he can, the increase in men and beasts over time makes it inevitable that the commons will be overgrazed until it can no longer support even one animal. Each man pursuing his own best interest inexorably works toward the ruin of all—a situation that Hardin describes as "the tragedy of the commons."

The inevitable tragedy of overuse has, in reality, affected many of our key environmental resources. Yet, when the damage resulting from the consumption of unpriced but valuable resources becomes a major social problem, as environmental damage has in recent years, the balance cannot readily be restored by creating private ownership rights. In most cases it is not physically possible to divide air, silence, and the like into marketable units, nor is it socially desirable to vest the use of environmental resources in pri-

vate hands. While direct regulation of use is the most obvious way
to deal with such a situation, the alternative of using market-
oriented pricing need not be discarded just because private ownership of resources is not possible. Legislatures could impose prices
on environmental resources and attempt to initiate, through legislative control, the functioning of the price mechanism in the mar-
ketplace. Scant attention has been given to this second avenue:
decentralized, market-oriented approaches to solving environmental
problems. It is unfortunate that this avenue remains essentially
unexplored, since even this brief discussion should have made it
clear that environmental damage and the economy are closely related and that economic analysis offers many insights into the causes
of environmental decay.[2]

Ideally, in implementing the charges, a legislature or agency
should impose on an environmentally damaging activity all of the
complex social costs that the activity incurs. The activity would
then pay for the resources it consumes, like any other economic
activity. Since computing total social damages poses enormous
practical difficulties, it will probably not be possible to attain this
ideal. However, given a legislatively determined level of environmental quality as a goal, the average costs of controlling environmental harms in various industries could be used to design a
charge that achieves a high level of efficiency, even if it does not
perfectly reflect all of an activity's social costs. Chapter 2 explains
how this works. While this approach requires moderately complex
economic analysis to identify charge levels that will cause industries and other institutions to control environmental degradation
to the desired degree, it is not impractical. The same approach can

---

[2] A market-oriented approach akin to charges which we will not be discussing,
but which has many theoretical virtues, was developed by J. H. Dales, who in 1970
proposed the generation of a market in pollution rights in *Pollution, Property and
Prices* (Toronto, University of Toronto, paperback ed., 1970) pp. 93–100. A plan for
implementing a marketable fixed-term discharge permit system was proposed by
H. D. Jacoby and G. W. Schaumburg in 1971, in E. I. Selig, ed., *Effluent Charges on
Air and Water Pollution: A Conference Report* 36-43 (Washington, Environmental
Law Institute, 1971). The concept of determining total permissible pollution and
auctioning off rights to pollute to that level has current champions. See Marc
Roberts and M. Spence, *Effluent Charges and Licenses Under Uncertainty*, Tech-
nical Rept. No. 146 (Institute for Mathematical Studies in the Social Sciences, Stan-
ford University, 1974); Marc Roberts and Richard Stewart, book review, *Harvard
Law Review* vol. 88 (1975) pp. 1644, 1653–54.

be applied to the environmentally harmful activities of individuals. The imposition of charges on throwaway containers and other solid wastes, on congestion, road use and the like, requires an identification of the level of economic incentive that will move individuals to respond in the socially desired way—an inquiry that may in the final analysis be a sociological inquiry as much as it is an economic one.

By emphasizing the economic aspects of environmental problems, we do not want to imply that *all* the causes of environmental degradation and the failure to cope with it are economic. Political, technical, cultural, legal, and other influences have contributed heavily to the current dilemma.[3] We also subscribe to the view that the ethic of consumption held by most Americans, a decidedly nondisciplinary, nonanalytic consideration, lies at the base of many of our environmental problems. Today, some feel that we may be overburdening our common resources for a dubious prosperity— oversized automobiles and highways, supersonic travel, space-age cosmetics, a Pandora's box of synthetic food dyes, and packaging materials and plastics that are nondegradable.

Charges and Compromise

Although we think charges are a promising environmental management strategy, we must point out that, as with many complex

[3] Some may think that we still have not taken enough perspectives into account. They are probably right, although it is difficult to know where to draw the line to keep interdisciplinary analyses to a manageable size. For example, Aaron Wildavsky, in reviewing an excellent interdisciplinary analysis of why the Delaware River clean-up effort has failed, gently chides the authors for not recognizing that the nation's high, expensive (the authors and economists would say "irrational") environmental goals may be grounded on a new level of rationality, in which economic cost–benefit comparisons have limited value. "Who . . . deals with decidedly different schemes of values? Anthropologists, obviously. About all Ackerman et al. leave out is anthropology—purification rites and pollution taboos. And that, I must say, in as broad a counsel of perfection as can be offered, is too bad. The outlandish behavior the authors record, behavior that is intendedly rational but functionally absurd, is not at all well explained by economic profit or political gain or technical imperatives or organizational abuses or legal hubris, although each of these explanations has merit in its own sphere, rather like an unfinished skyscraper whose spaces are illuminated at night but whose superstructure—the grid that gives groups of spaces their meaning—is blacked out." (Review of Bruce A. Ackerman, Susan Rose Ackerman, James W. Sawyer, Jr., and Dale W. Henderson, *The Uncertain Search for Environmental Quality* in *Stanford Law Review* vol. 29 (1976) p. 183.)

social controls, workable charges plans will require some important compromises between theory and reality. One such compromise has already been identified above: as a practical matter total social damages are almost impossible to compute. What is the value of clean air to a citizen at the city center? One mile from the city center? Ten? How can these be added together? The value of *clean* air is theoretically easier to compute than the value of *clear* air: what is the money value of a clear view to citizens at varying distances from the city center? How can these be added? It would obviously be very difficult to base a charge on total social harms. Yet, computing and imposing such a charge would place the right price on our environmental resources.

In this dilemma, a compromise with economic theory will have to be made if viable legislation is to be designed for the charges approach. Chapter 3 shows how far we can retreat from pure economic theory and still reap major benefits from charges. The workable charges schemes we envision are not perfect; they would not impose exactly the right price on environmental resources in perfectly functioning markets. Rather, charges would be used to achieve predetermined environmental standards and would be based upon a rough and ready estimate either of the costs of environmental control of various industries, services, and municipalities, or upon an estimate, somewhat sociological in nature, of the charge that will induce citizens and consumers to modify their behavior.

An additional, troublesome problem arises because many markets are resistant to purely economic incentives because of rate structures and profits guaranteed by heavy government regulation. Finally, some economists doubt that businesses in our economy are guided by the kind of pure economic rationality hypothesized in economic theory. If they are not, charges may not have their desired full effect.

We want to be candid about these difficulties from the outset, so that the reader understands that we make our arguments for charges in awareness of their possible shortcomings. Environmental control of any type is necessarily a very complex endeavor. Any environmental control strategy must be fair to multiple and conflicting legitimate interests, will be based on imperfect data, and must take into account the vagaries of the modern mixed economy. Every control strategy forwarded surely can be criticized on many grounds. Charges cannot escape such criticism. Charges

will not function perfectly from an economic point of view, nor
will they be totally free of technical, administrative, legal, and
political difficulty. But charges compare favorably with direct regulation in so many key ways that they deserve serious attention.

Charges and Direct Regulation

All environmental programs have to pass through the same law-
making process. In comparing charges with direct regulation, we
must not forget that many attributes, and difficulties, will be common to both approaches. Legislative politics will take their toll of
charges and direct regulation alike. A legislature, whether local,
state, or federal, must take all the steps necessary to enact a valid
law establishing the control program. The law must satisfy the
courts, if it is challenged, that its provisions lie within the permissible limits of legislative power expressed in federal and state constitutions. A fairly extensive administrative infrastructure will
have to be created to administer any program. All programs will
involve a considerable bureaucracy, additional rule making by the
regulatory agency, and judicial oversight by the courts to assure
that the legislative intent is obeyed and individual rights are not
infringed. Finally, all programs require that discharges and ambient quality be monitored; there is no escaping this technological
imperative. Hence, all control programs will share certain legislative, administrative, technical, and judicial aspects.

Ambient and Effluent Standards

Within this common framework, however, a great deal of variety
is possible in the amount of emphasis different schemes place on
the roles of the legislature, the agencies, and the courts. In most
important environmental control programs in the United States,
heavy reliance is placed upon direct regulation by administrative
agencies, backed up by frequent judicial review in the courts.
Under the federal Clean Air Act and Water Pollution Control
Act, agencies set standards for the amount of pollutants that can
be released to the environment and police the implementation of
these standards by the states. Two types of standards are typically
involved. The first type, the ambient standard, is a legal specifica-

tion of minimum conditions which must be met for some indicator of environmental quality at a specified location in one of the environmental media. For example, an ambient standard may state that dissolved oxygen, averaged over a 24-hour period at a selected river mile point, must not fall below 4 parts per million more than one day per year. The second type, the effluent standard, specifies a mean or maximum permissible discharge of a pollutant from a single, particular source. For example, Ajax Corporation Plant Number One may not discharge more than a set number of pounds of sulfur oxides per day. Effluent standards are requirements (either by weight of materials or concentrations) set on the quality characteristics of the actual discharges. Ambient standards refer to quality requirements for the receiving watercourse or airshed. Ambient and effluent standards are not mutually exclusive and coexist in control programs today. In the case of water pollution, use of both standards is coupled with a massive federal subsidy program for construction of waste treatment facilities.

Direct regulation, relying heavily upon centralized standard setting and enforcement, is vulnerable to inefficiency, enforcement difficulties, and unpenalized delay. As Ward Elliott has remarked, "direct regulation is geared to the pace of the slowest and the strength of the weakest."[4] The shortsightedness of current programs suggests beginning a search for programs which emphasize more than end-of-pipe controls, capital-intensive solutions brought about by massive subsidies, and technical standard setting for a variety of sources of environmental harm by large federal and state bureaucracies.

Cost Effectiveness

Perhaps the most frequently used argument in favor of adopting charges rather than direct regulatory approaches is that charges are more cost effective. The comparison of the two approaches on these grounds is important, because the greater the cost effectiveness of the approach adopted, the lower the total bill that society must pay for the achievement of environmental standards.

[4] Private communication to Thomas Quinn, Air Resources Board, Sacramento, California, from Ward Elliott, Associate Professor of Political Science, Claremont Men's College, Claremont, California, September 2, 1976.

Different types of dischargers of the same pollutant may have to spend widely divergent amounts to reduce their discharges to a given level. For instance, sugar beet manufacturers control discharges of biological oxygen demand (BOD) more cheaply than steel makers at almost all levels of control. Furthermore, control costs vary significantly even among individual sugar beet firms. Thus the total cost of a given level of pollutant reduction can vary widely, depending on how the cleanup burden is allocated among individual sources. If, for instance, all sources are required to control discharges to the same extent, total costs may be far greater than necessary to achieve a preselected level of ambient environmental quality.

It is vitally important to reduce the total costs of pollution control wherever possible because the sums involved are so staggering. For example, the National Commission on Water Quality has put the capital cost of achieving the statutorily mandated "best available technology" by 1983 at $43 billion. Thus pollution control by direct regulation could cause a significant shift in national spending patterns, which suggests that less costly solutions should be sought to avoid the risk of a congressional scaling down of the pollution control effort. Charges approaches could help avoid this outcome, because they require fewer real resources than current pollution control schemes in order to achieve the same degree of ambient quality.

Charges systems are a cost-effective means of achieving environmental quality goals because, with charges, each source decides how much to control on the basis of its own control costs. Thus, sources whose costs of control are high will control less; those with low costs will control more. The logical net result is that the average cost of control per unit of pollutant would be lower than it would be under regulatory schemes that do not allow this type of private decision making to take place. With charges, the cost of environmental cleanup is less for the overall economy.

In examining the advantages of charges we do not want to overstate the economic shortcomings of the regulatory approach. In certain ways current approaches to air and water pollution control do take economics into account. In the actual implementation of the air and water pollution control acts, federal and state officials are striving to achieve a better economic result, primarily by tak-

ing into account differences in control costs among different categories and subcategories of sources. However, their purpose is not achievement of economic, or market, efficiency as such, and it is not yet clear exactly what the result is in terms of this criterion. Under the Federal Clean Air Act, performance standards for new stationary sources take control costs into account and differentiate among the relative abilities of industrial subcategories to control emissions. In their detailed plans to implement nationwide ambient standards, states can take individual existing sources' relative economic ability to control emissions into account, so long as overall federally mandated ambient quality levels are achieved. These results are defensible on economic grounds. We are not aware, however, of efforts directed explicitly to achieving economically efficient results, and we suspect that the local polluters' political and legal strength usually overcomes any efforts to pursue such efficiency as a primary goal.

Under the Federal Water Pollution Control Act Amendments of 1972, both new and existing dischargers are subject to effluent guidelines which are based on technological considerations and economic analyses. The economic analyses take into account the costs different classes of sources face in meeting standards, and analyze the ability of different classes of sources to meet those costs. This approach, however, does not uniformly stimulate those polluters whose control costs are lowest to make the largest contribution to pollution control. Because there is no reason for the control costs for a class of sources and the existing economic strength of that class to be correlated either positively or negatively, the result is probably mixed in terms of cost effectiveness. Thus, sources in an industry subgroup that is generally in excellent economic health may well be required to achieve higher levels of control than sources in another subgroup of the same industry that is faltering economically, even if the latter faced lower costs per unit of control. However, an opposite tendency toward a more cost-effective result is just as likely to occur.

Without empirical data that allow a comparison of control levels required by the effluent guidelines for different types of sources with the control costs for those categories, it is not possible to assess accurately the cost effectiveness of the present approach. It does appear that it is somewhat more cost effective than a system

requiring equal discharge reductions from all sources of a given pollutant. The current approach tends toward cost effectiveness within groups of industries in equivalent financial condition that have similar control options, because the relative control levels required of those industries are determined by the costs of control.

One point related to the cost effectiveness of the current system need not rest, however, on empirical assessment of existing programs. To the extent that current systems function properly, administrators force industry subgroups and individual dischargers to do their utmost within their widely varying economic and technical abilities to control pollution. Unfortunately, this approach assumes that existing product lines can continue to be produced in the way they always have been and that once dischargers have done all they can to control discharges through conventional means, they will not have to close plants or lay off employees. An efficient approach would require dischargers to accept the full economic consequences of using valuable resources such as clean air and water. If the total cost of cleaning up discharges to the air and water plus other conventionally priced production process inputs is greater than the income which the output generates, a company would fail, but the failure would be part of a desirable readjustment toward greater market efficiency.

Enforcement

The major problem with standards-based regulatory programs is not that they in theory are incapable of achieving cost-effective or economically efficient results, but that in practice they could do so only at enormous administrative costs. Current approaches require setting standards based on careful economic analyses of entire polluting industries, mastering the technologies of production and pollution control in the regulated industries, and elaborately subcategorizing industrial processes which are sufficiently different to merit different pollution control standards. The standards arrived at through these involved procedures are often challenged in court on the grounds that they do not represent the "best practicable control technology currently available" or the appropriate statutory standard. The court tests often bog down in

debates on arcane technical questions that courts are ill-equipped to resolve. The process of applying the standards to individual sources, as in drafting permits for National Pollution Discharge Emission System, consumes a great deal of time and administrative resources because it requires negotiation over the specific characteristics of each source. Finally, the standards in the permit must be enforced, another process replete with administrative and legal tangles. All of these tasks are made more difficult by the complexity of the standards and the standard-setting process that is necessary to achieve economic objectives, whether they be minimization of plant closures, achievement of cost effectiveness, or overall market efficiency. Why this is so deserves closer attention.

Standard setting is not simply a process of telling a polluter what emission standards he must meet, and then monitoring his emissions to see if he has complied. As we have said, under most legislative provisions, standards pass through some type of benefit–cost comparison—they must be "practical" or "available," or technically and economically "feasible." These are elastic terms intended to make the environmental control agency justify its standards as technologically proven and nonbankrupting. Naturally, there is considerable room for debate over whether an abatement process is really "feasible," and the burden on the agency is increased still further by the requirement that the standards take into account relevant differences in an industry. Thus, what is a feasible and practicable abatement technique for one firm in an industry may not be so for another plant in the same industry, depending on the plant's technology, its rate of return on investment, and other plant-specific factors.

Data on the abatement alternatives open to a polluter, of course, are best known to the polluter himself in most cases, or at least to the subcontractor hired by him. It is difficult for an outsider to an industry to know what the real possibilities are, because there are often few outsiders doing research into abatement or employing full-scale abatement techniques.

Then, too, even if he performs the research, or depends upon a control technology subindustry, the polluter has every incentive not to share this information with a regulatory agency, for then the agency will augment the standards to reduce discharges further, or

be less hesitant about cracking down on violators. There is no
incentive to perform research which serves in the end to increase
a company's capital outlays, with no increase in profits. As yet,
there is little evidence that the subcontractors who build control
systems will come forward to share their technological advances.

Without accurate or accurate-appearing information on abatement techniques, a regulatory agency is in a bind. It cannot require an industry or firm to do something that is impossible, yet
it does not know the limits of the possible. The agency's dilemma
is particularly troublesome when there is no viable abatement
technique available. It cannot know what several years of highly
motivated research and development would turn up, yet it has not
been provided with techniques for making dischargers conduct
vigorous research programs. If an agency decides to be strict and
impose standards that an industry thinks cannot be met, it must
fight industry experts in administrative proceedings and in court.
It cannot, of course, fathom the outcome of these enforcement
proceedings in advance. Hence, under direct regulation, an agency
is required to make and defend decisions on the technological
alternatives available to a polluting firm or industry, with all that
this involves in terms of detailed knowledge of each industry's
technologies and economics. The control agency cannot be expected to have the best expertise in the country on the technological alternatives facing every firm or industry; polluters will
almost always know more about their own operations and alternatives than an environmental agency can ever hope to learn. Yet,
under a regulatory system, this is precisely the kind of knowledge
an environmental control agency must have in order to enforce
standards.

Under a system of monetary charges, after the basic charge rate
is decided, the greatest source of continuing debate between polluters and the agency concerns, not the technical alternatives
available for abatement, but the devices and procedures used to
monitor the quantity and quality of the pollutants discharged.
Administrative expertise is directed to monitoring technologies.
This is a highly favorable turnabout, because it is much more
reasonable to expect the U.S. Environmental Protection Agency
(EPA) or a state agency to become the recognized authority on

monitoring procedures than to expect it to become knowledgeable
about every production and pollution control technology in use or
soon to be feasible.

Of course, in setting charges the legislature or agency must have
at its disposal approximate estimates, prepared as carefully as possible, of the costs of controlling each type of pollution or other
activity covered by the legislation. This initial information requirement goes beyond the needs of monitoring; however, this type of
information is useful and necessary in any event before a legislature or agency can make any decision about control strategies
that take costs into account.

The imposing requirements for technical information under the
regulatory approach might be less troublesome if polluters had
some incentive to abate their discharges even before all the information was in; in the absence of such incentives, direct regulation
is *doubly* handicapped. Consider the incentives for a typical polluting firm. On the one hand, if the polluter complies with the
applicable standards, he must meet the annualized expenses of installing and operating expensive abatement equipment. He also
faces a shift in competitive position that is less easily calculated,
for he cannot be sure that his competitors will face the same added
abatement costs. On the other hand, if the firm does not comply,
it will incur costs only if it is caught by the enforcing agency. The
expected value of these costs equals the probability of being sin-
gled out for prosecution, times the cost of the ensuing legal and
political fight, plus the product of the probability of losing a court
case and incurring the sanctions likely to be imposed.

Since it is only one among thousands of firms, an individual
company normally has no great expectation of being among the
relatively few selected for vigorous attention by a regulatory agency.
And, it may also reason, if a successful crackdown appears likely in
its area, it will probably be possible to negotiate a new compliance
schedule with a pollution control agency that is more eager to gain
voluntary compliance than to expend its resources in protracted
administrative and judicial battles. Moreover, where its abatement
options are expensive and of doubtful reliability, a firm can reasonably expect to make a convincing case in court about the in-
feasibility or unreasonableness of the agency's emission require-

ments. At the very least, it can avoid presenting a case so flimsy that a judge will react punitively. What is probably most defeating to the direct regulation strategy, however, are the long, unpenalized delays in compliance which a firm can enjoy by simply dragging its feet throughout the protracted enforcement process. The polluter pays nothing for the emissions it discharges while the legal and political processes run their course. The more abatement costs a firm, and the more doubtful the existence of a "feasible" abatement option, the greater the incentive to fight the regulatory agency each step of the way.

American legal institutions are usually designed to deal with only a small percentage of potential violators. Voluntary compliance is assumed, and generally forthcoming. Under the regulatory approach, however, the benefits of delay are typically so great in comparison with the costs of complying that there is little incentive for voluntary compliance, and a regulatory agency faces the possibility, not of a handful of violators that it could reasonably and effectively handle, but of tacit noncompliance by large segments of an industry. At this point the regulatory process stalls as the enforcement agency begins to bargain with polluters over what equipment to install and what constitutes compliance, to accept a minimum level of emission reductions, and to celebrate these weak, negotiated standards as proof of agency vigilance and success, rather than admit failure publicly and go to the legislature to seek a more effective solution. The agency is slowly and relentlessly coerced toward industry's standards, rather than its own.

In theory, these defects could be compensated for by giving the agency many more scientists, engineers, and lawyers, by making the penalties for proven violations more credible or more severe, by changing the elastic nature of the "feasibility" criteria, and by mounting massive parallel research programs to learn even more about industrial production processes and abatement technologies.

In practice, however, the political and economic costs of a fully effective program of direct regulation are simply too high. Legislatures are, wisely, unwilling to scuttle judicial protections against arbitrary decisions by governmental agencies just to compensate for the shortcomings of direct regulation. Nor do they want to create the large and expensive bureaucracies that would be re-

quired for effective enforcement of environmental standards. In times of particular public concern over environmental matters, the result tends to be the kind of legislative overreaction that manifests itself in seemingly "tough" but unrealistic standards with no means of implementation.

A charge system, by contrast, requires fewer enforcement tools because it changes the incentive structure facing the polluter. Delay no longer pays: a firm is charged for the damage it causes to the environment even while administrative or judicial challenges are underway. The continuous financial pressure of the charges can be relieved only by the abatement of the environmental harm. Even if it wishes to delay, a firm is no longer in a position to argue with a regulatory agency over the technical and economic feasibility of its abatement options; they are now irrelevant. Once the charge is set, the firm's only concern becomes to choose the most economically efficient abatement alternative. And, since it will continue to pay a charge for whatever it continues to discharge, the firm will have an incentive to search for improved abatement techniques to reduce its charge payments in the future. The effect of charges is to turn the energies of a firm from attempts to outmaneuver a regulatory agency to efforts to develop cheaper, more effective means of lessening the environmental damage it causes.

Although charges are still largely untried, they could be a useful adjunct to and in some cases might be superior to direct regulation as a strategy for controlling environmental problems. But this cannot be known for sure until they have been tried. We do not want to imply, moreover, in anything we have written, that the two strategies are mutually antagonistic or inconsistent. Many practical plans for charges in fact call for the meshing of the two approaches (see chapter 3). Some environmental problems, such as the control of toxic substances, are not amenable to a charges approach and must be directly regulated, usually to achieve zero discharges. In other cases, a charge may be used as an additional incentive to attain a predetermined discharge level, but may not apply to emissions below that level. In Connecticut, charges were recently used within a regulatory system to remove the incentive for polluters to delay compliance with discharge standards. The possibilities for combinations of the two approaches are virtually

limitless. In the remaining chapters we will mention from time to time circumstances where a combination of the two approaches seems appropriate.

Other Incentives

While there appear to be possibilities for introducing the charges concept into the arsenal of environmental control strategies, and for coordinating charges and direct regulatory systems, there is one form of "economic incentive," sometimes praised for its potential role in improving environmental quality, which should be considered before leaving this chapter.

Incentives that have been mentioned in connection with environmental management have included devices such as tax breaks or low interest loans for the construction of treatment facilities. While it is part of an economic approach to environmental control, this sort of "incentive" is of a wholly different nature from the charges which are discussed here (these could, however, be called "negative incentives"). Even if such incentives induce investment in pollution control facilities, they are an economically inefficient means of reducing pollution, amounting to no more than a subsidy to producers and consumers of the affected products.

Accelerated depreciation and tax credits, or even grants to meet part of the construction cost of facilities, will not, by themselves, cause reductions in discharges to the environment. They merely reduce losses on waste treatment equipment; they do not make the installation of that equipment profitable. In other words, no firm or local government acting rationally would provide any treatment solely because it is offered this kind of incentive. Subsidies may "sweeten" a control program, but they can never replace it.

Furthermore, all proposals for tax breaks or other forms of subsidy that have come to our attention provide incentives only for investment in treatment equipment. In many cases the most efficient way to reduce discharges is to alter production processes, recover materials, produce marketable goods from by-products, or change the nature or quality of the raw materials. In numerous instances, process changes (use of savealls in paper production,

black liquor recovery in pulp production, syrup recovery in canning, and so on) result in both waste reduction and recovery of valuable materials. By providing no incentive for process-related changes, subsidies tend to distort investment decisions toward treatment of wastes after they are generated. Even where they do stimulate investment in the most efficient means of reducing discharges, these proposals do not pass muster. If these incentives were widely introduced, their administration would become extremely complex because of the intimate relationship between production processes and the wastes produced. Without careful policing of individual plants, it would be virtually impossible to distinguish costs incurred to reduce waste loads from costs incurred to increase the profitability of industrial processes. Moreover, the availability of subsidies for treatment facilities would substantially lessen the incentive of a firm or industry to develop new, more efficient means of reducing discharges.

Finally, tax writeoffs and credits would probably not benefit marginally profitable firms, which might have to close down if effective controls are imposed, because the subsidies only partially alleviate pollution control costs. This is ironic because these devices are often justified as protection for the small firm. They protect the small firm just as effectively as our agricultural programs protect the small farm. If real protection is warranted, a more narrowly targeted system must be developed.

In addition to the factors just discussed, subsidy programs are a drain on the federal treasury and on a tax system which many feel is already overworked. In contrast, charges can yield revenue while improving the allocation of resources.

In the pages that follow, this caution should be kept in mind: beyond certain general characteristics, each environmental problem has its own features, deriving from such factors as the specific nature of the local or state economy; the number, size, and influence of sources of environmental harm; the technical alternatives available to control environmental damage and the costs of damage; the likely final incidences of these costs; and the authority of the control agency. This means that each charge proposal must be designed and analyzed in light of the particular characteristics of a given situation. Our goal is not to describe all these possibilities, but rather to make explicit the pros and cons of the major

types of charges systems. We recognize that the political process and skillful legislative drafting may come up with innovations that make acceptable some aspect of a charge system that at present appears to be undesirable. They may also find intolerable some other aspect that currently seems perfectly acceptable. There is no way to foresee any of this. But we think that careful attention to what we perceive as the major issues will be helpful to those who must develop or react to concrete legislative proposals.

2

An Economic Rationale

for Charges

From an economist's point of view, the primary purpose of environmental charge systems is to establish new markets that efficiently allocate environmental resources. The lack of such markets is a major cause of environmental problems. Manufacturers dump raw wastes into the air and water without regard to the high social costs of such action, not because they are bad people, but because it is economically advantageous for them to do so. Their use of other resources is subject to market prices and constraints; their use of these environmental resources is not. Similar incentives encourage commuters to drive into crowded, smog-blanketed cities alone in their cars. A commuter bears costs in terms of delay, noise, and health effects that are small compared to the total societal costs of accommodating the additional motorist. Similar problems are found wherever environmental resources are outside the existing market system.

The preceding chapter touched on the economic reasons for this kind of individually rational, but collectively irrational, behavior. This chapter explains more fully how the market system should work to allocate resources, why it does not work for environmental resources, and why and how charges could remedy the problem.[1]

---

[1] Our discussion is limited to the more general aspects of the economics underlying charges. For a more detailed analysis of the economic theory and political aspects of charges, see *The Polluter Pays Principle*, prepared for the Organisation for Economic Co-operation and Development (Paris, 1975).

The Market System and the Allocation of Resources

Resources are the basic inputs of production and consumption processes. One of the more noteworthy achievements of the classical economists was the demonstration that whenever certain basic assumptions are satisfied, the freely functioning market system will use all resources efficiently. That is, as stated in chapter 1, more of one good cannot be produced without reducing the production of some other good, and one individual cannot be given more of any good without someone else getting less.

The success of the market system in allocating resources efficiently depends upon the maximization of individual self-interests by producers and consumers. A firm will pick that output or combination of outputs which maximizes its profits. Similarly, consumers allocate their incomes so that they acquire the greatest total satisfaction from the bundle of goods which is consumed.

In order that the maximization of individual self-interest lead to the efficient allocation of resources, four basic assumptions must be satisfied. First, the individual units of production and consumption must be small compared to the overall size of each market; economists refer to this as a competitive situation. (By way of contrast, when one unit of production controls all output in a market, a monopoly situation exists.) Second, producers and consumers must be fully informed as to present and future prices. Third, there must be no externalities; that is, the activities of an individual economic agent acting alone must not affect the costs or satisfaction experienced by another. Fourth, there must be free entry into a profitable activity and free exit from an unprofitable activity. In reality, none of these assumptions is fully satisfied in a typical market economy. This book concentrates on the third assumption, that there should be no externalities, and the implications for public policy when this assumption is not satisfied.

Externalities frequently lead to a breakdown in the performance of market mechanisms. Externalities have obvious visible effects on that class of nonmarket goods known as environmental amenities—clean air, clean water, peace and quiet, and open space. They affect the allocation of many other goods and services, including the harvest of fish from the oceans, traffic flow on urban highways, and the production of petroleum from jointly owned pools.

Table 1
(Profit Obtained with Various Fertilizer Inputs)

1 Fertilizer tons per acre	2 Fertilizer cost	3 Total cost	4 Marginal factor cost	5 Bushels of wheat per acre	6 Total revenue	7 Marginal revenue product	8 Profit
0	0	65	0	25	75		10
1	10	75	10	30	90	15	15
2	15	80	5	33	99	9	19
3	20	85	5	35	105	6	20
4	25	90	5	36	108	3	18

In a competitive market setting with many producers and consumers, an individual producer or consumer has no control over the key cog in the system, the prices of goods and services. Each individual producer or consumer pays the market price for those things he wishes to purchase and accepts the market price for those things he wishes to sell. It is easy to see that a producer will decide how much of his products to make by comparing the market price for those products with the costs of production. Consider a farmer engaged in the production of wheat. Suppose the principal variable under the control of the farmer is the amount of fertilizer that he will apply to his fixed quantity of land. (Labor, seed, machinery, and other inputs are assumed fixed.) Table 1 depicts the relevant data for the farmer.

Let us assume that the cost of applying fertilizer consists of a fixed cost of application of $5 per acre, plus $5 for each ton of fertilizer used. Other costs of operation, such as labor, taxes, seed, and insurance, amount to $65 per acre. Wheat is sold for $3 per bushel.

The profit-maximizing farmer will increase his use of fertilizer until profits reach a maximum. This occurs when 3 tons of fertilizer are used and a profit of $20 per acre is earned (columns 1 and 8). Notice that profits increase as long as the costs associated with the use of each additional ton of fertilizer fall short of the corresponding gain in revenue contributed by the ton of fertilizer. Economists term the incremental cost of the fertilizer its marginal factor cost (column 4), and the incremental increase in revenue the marginal revenue product (or equivalently, the value of the

marginal product of the fertilizer) (column 7). Technically then, more of an input is purchased until the marginal cost of the input, which is just the input price in a competitive market setting, equals the marginal revenue product derived from the input (columns 4 and 7).

When all users of fertilizer make similar profit-maximizing calculations, the total available supply of fertilizer is said to be allocated efficiently. For each farmer, or other user of fertilizer, the last units applied bring forth a quantity of additional output just equal to the value of fertilizer which is used. There would be no way to reallocate fertilizer applications to produce outputs which would have a higher value to society.[2]

Now let us turn to the issue of externalities. Suppose that the farmer's fertilizer does not all remain in the soil, that in fact some of it dissolves in runoff from heavy rains and pollutes downstream water supplies. Suppose that the downstream pollution caused by the fertilizer in the runoff costs the users of the water supply approximately $3 for every ton of fertilizer applied to each acre. Because the farmer does not pay this cost, he does not factor the $3 into his profit-maximizing computations. The consequence is that from the viewpoint of society as a whole, too much fertilizer is being used. If the farmer were made to pay the pollution cost of runoff contaminated with fertilizer, for instance, if the stream were private property and he had to pay legal damages, he would use less fertilizer. As shown in table 2, the marginal factor cost of each ton of fertilizer used would be increased from 5 to 8. Since the marginal revenue product from the second ton (9) is greater than the marginal cost, but the marginal revenue from the third ton (6) is less, the farmer's optimal use would be only 2 tons per acre. The third ton yields the farmer a private profit of $1,

[2] This situation is often referred to as a "Pareto optimum," named for Vilfredo Pareto, a prominent Italian economist and social theoretician. Pareto optimality has been demonstrated to result from exchange in theoretical, competitive market models which contain labor markets, markets for raw materials, markets for intermediate goods, and markets for consumer goods; in other words, for a reasonably complete if highly abstract characterization of the functions performed in an actual economy. The basic paper is by K. J. Arrow and G. Debreu, "Existence of an Equilibrium for a Competitive Economy," *Econometrica* vol. 22, no. 3 (1954). A summary of the literature is printed in Hukukane Nikaido, *Convex Structures in Economic Theory* (New York, Academic Press, 1968).

Table 2
(Costs and Revenues with External Costs Internalized)

1	2	3	4	5	6	7	8
Fertilizer tons per acre	Fertilizer cost	Total cost	Marginal factor cost	Bushels of wheat per acre	Total revenue	Marginal revenue product	Profit
0	0	65		25	75		10
1	13	78	13	30	90	15	12
2	21	86	8	33	99	9	13
3	29	94	8	35	105	6	11
4	37	102	8	36	108	3	6

but when a charge equal to the extra social cost of pollution is added, he would incur a loss of $2 on the third ton.

As we have seen from table 1, with fertilizer at $5 a ton, the farmer's profit is maximized at 3 tons of fertilizer per acre. The social damage, or externalities, of using this amount of fertilizer is $9 (3 tons × $3 damages per ton); therefore the net social benefit is $11 ($20 per acre profit − $9 damage). When a pollution tax is added to the fertilizer cost, bringing it up to $8 per ton, the farmer's profit is maximized at 2 tons of fertilizer per acre and the social damage is reduced to $6 (table 2). The tax revenue yielded on 2 tons of fertilizer is $6 and the net social benefit is thus $13 ($13 profit − $6 social damage + $6 tax). Thus a pollution tax of $3 per ton of fertilizer encourages the farmer to reduce his use of fertilizer by 1 ton and produces a social gain of $2, an optimal result. Who enjoys the gain depends on how the tax revenues are distributed. The problem of the use of charge revenues is discussed in chapter 6, and chapter 3 describes how some countries have allocated the funds derived from charge-oriented systems.

Bringing Resources into the Market System

Environmental resources are often overused because the costs of their use are not taken into account in production costs. Waste disposal services should be considered as inputs to production if environmental resources are to be subject to market processes. While it may not benefit the farmer to have fertilizer washed away in stormwater runoff, it does benefit him when the same thing

happens to the wastes from his feedlots. Similarly, the disposal of factory wastes can be viewed as a productive service. Where there is no charge for dumping wastes into rivers, the air, or vacant land, factories and individuals alike will rely heavily on these means of getting rid of the useless residues from their production processes. If a good such as fertilizer were free, farmers would use it until it was no longer profitable to do so. Where natural waste disposal services are free, farmers and others will use them until they have exhausted all the marginal benefits.

Of course, the fact that the farmer does not pay when storm-water carries off feedlot wastes, and the factory does not pay when particulates, sulfur oxides, and other wastes are emitted into the atmosphere, does not mean that no one pays. The external costs of such uses are paid by other members of society. Just as those using stream water below a farm bear the costs of the pollution from fertilizer runoff, so those downwind of a factory bear the costs of its air pollution. And these costs nowhere enter into the profit and loss calculations of economic enterprises, which get their signals and incentives from prices determined by market exchange.[3]

Many environmental resources have never been subject to the allocation process of the market system. In most cases, these resources were once so plentiful that there was little or no cost generated by their use and therefore no need for a distributive mechanism. However, even when these resources became scarce, they were not brought into the market system and, as discussed in chapter 1, remain as common property resources.

In the absence of effective governmental restrictions, such common property resources as air and water, for example, tend to be used as free goods. As we saw earlier, individual action based on self-interest does not serve the social good, but perversely drives groups to waste and often eventually to ruin their common property. No individual user has any incentive to limit his use or to upgrade the

---

[3] All of this having been said, it should be pointed out that not all uses of environmental resources are necessarily destructive. Animals, including ourselves, breathing the air, and even combustion processes, do not normally deplete oxygen to an extent that measurably affects the breathing of others or other combustion processes. A person viewing a landscape does not diminish its beauty (unless the viewers themselves become an unwanted part of the landscape).

resource. The individual would have to bear all the costs of such action, and for many types of pollution problems these costs can be quite large. In addition, there would be no assurance that there would be any benefits; others might simply intensify their consumption of the resource. Even if there were benefits, they would be divided among all the common "owners," and the individual "conservationist" would reap only a small portion of them.

From careful study of particular common property problems such as oil pools and ocean fisheries, it is well established that unhindered access to such resources leads to overuse, misuse, and general loss of environmental quality. In the case of pollution, this takes the form of large masses of materials and energy discharged to watercourses, land, and the atmosphere, degrading their quality.

One response to the inability of market systems to allocate environmental resources is government management of the use of those resources. As discussed in chapter 1, government regulation is the primary management approach used in this country. Government sets standards designed to limit everyone's consumption of environmental resources. These standards are based on the technical limits of pollution cleanup, the costs of the cleanup, and on environmental goals. Government then polices the use of the resources in an attempt to make sure that the standards are met. The absence of the economic incentives of the market is remedied by the coercive power of the state. However, this is not the only means available.

If we could stretch our minds and envisage a situation where common property resources could be reduced to private ownership in pieces small enough to be exchanged in competitive markets, then, distributional issues aside, the market could function just as efficiently to allocate them as any other resource. Those for whom environmental resources were valuable or productive, whether for waste disposal, commercial use such as fishing, or recreation, would purchase units of them. The resources would be used by each such entity up to the point at which the value of the marginal product equaled the input price, value of the marginal product being the change in the value of total product that results from one additional unit of input, all other inputs being constant. Another economic concept, opportunity cost, then enters the picture. The

opportunity cost of a resource or good is the value that is forgone when that good is put to one use rather than another. It is the value of the resource in the next most productive use to which it could have been applied. If environmental resources were priced and used in an economically rational manner, their prices would indicate their opportunity costs and would affect a whole complex of decisions about their use—the design of industrial processes, the kinds and amounts of raw materials used, the nature of the final products produced, and the modification of pollution streams. These resources would be used in a way that produced a net benefit for society instead of being destructively overused.

Pricing the Use of the Environment: Three Approaches

If bringing the environment into the market system could, in principle, yield such desirable results, why not try to define property rights to environmental media by governmental action, remove them from common property status, and let the market take over? Just as ownership of entities like corporations, which are not readily divisible into small units, is represented by paper shares to render it more easily marketable, so ownership of environmental resources could be broken into similarly artificial units. For instance, a total limit could be set for discharges of a given substance in a given area. The total allowable discharge could be broken up into units, for example, 100 pounds per year. The problem would then become how to distribute these discharge rights.

One way of allocating these pollution rights would be to distribute them to persons who might be disadvantaged by environmental deterioration and then require those wishing to engage in an environmentally degrading activity to purchase or lease the rights from these owners. Some writers consider this approach feasible.[4] Others do not. We are among the skeptics. How are the

---

[4] See, for instance, J. H. Dales, *Pollution, Property and Prices* (Toronto, University of Toronto Press, 1968). See also the discussion of the proposals by Henry Jacoby and Grant Schaumburg in Edward Selig, ed., *Effluent Charges on Air and Water Pollution*, monograph series no. 1 (Washington, Environmental Law Institute, 1973) pp. 36–43.

appropriate owners to be identified and what share of rights are they to be given? Is the New Mexican who occasionally comes to New York City to be accorded a piece of New York's air? How could the purchaser who wishes to use the environment find and pay each of the thousands, if not millions, of people involved? The costs, sometimes called transaction costs, of creating a market in this way would be enormous.

Since the disturbers of environmental quality are often small in number relative to affected parties (litterers and motorists are notable exceptions), it has sometimes been suggested that ownership rights be vested in them. Unfortunately, this second approach does not appear to be a workable way out either. It would be very difficult for the thousands of people in an area who would benefit from clean air, for instance, to purchase enough discharge rights to cause a meaningful improvement in air quality. Once again, we come up against transaction costs. In the absence of large-scale group action, this system would face common property problems. If one damaged party made such a payment, he would simultaneously benefit many others also damaged by the discharger. The benefit from improving the environment is the sum of damages done to many different individuals by the same discharge. Accordingly, the overall damage might be large relative to the costs of reduction, but the damage to one or even a sizable group of individuals is likely to be small compared to the reduction costs. An individual or small group would not find it in its interest to pay for the reduction. The importance of such problems may be gauged by considering the history of pollution control. In many instances governments have failed to protect the public interest in environmental resources, thus by default granting *de facto* ownership rights to the destructive user. Yet, there have been virtually no actual cases of damaged parties paying residuals dischargers to stop or reduce their discharge. Thus, a "paper" market in environmental resources is not very practical.

A third approach does make it possible to obtain many of the benefits of market allocation of air, water, and similar resources. Government can simply set prices or charges on all uses of such resources that create external costs. It could require those wishing to discharge pollutants into the air or water, or to mine or build in scenic areas, to fly noisy airplanes or to drive smog-breeding

cars into cities, to pay for these uses of the common property resources. Such charges, if carefully set, would have the same effect
as market prices on the choices of individuals wanting to consume
environmental resources. External costs would be internalized to
some degree.

The main difference between this approach and the market system is in the means by which the price level is determined. In the
market, prices are set by forces of supply and demand that represent the cumulative effect of thousands of individual decisions.
With an environmental charge, the price structure is set in a single
decision by government. The effect of the system will critically depend on how that choice is exercised.

How High a Price?

In principle, government should set the price on the destructive
uses of the environment on the basis of the amount of external cost
that those activities create. Charges based on external costs would,
under ideal circumstances, approximate the prices generated by a
purely competitive market for the resources. In practice, however,
this is not possible, and further on in this chapter, and indeed
throughout the rest of this book, we discuss modifications of this
principle which carry us further toward practical applicability
while still retaining many of the desirable theoretical features of
a price system.

Theoretically, the optimal price to levy on an environmentally
damaging activity is the price at which an increase in the cost of
discharge reduction is just equal to the decrease in damage that
results. If a lower charge rate were set, the resulting level of pollution control would not be optimal because an additional dollar
spent on control would reduce damages by more than a dollar. On
the other hand, if a higher charge were set, the costs of additional
control achieved would exceed the benefits. If the optimal price
level could be identified for each environmentally destructive activity, the result would be economically rational for the individual
and society. The market would aggregate the individual production and consumption activities into supply and demand forces
that would take into account both the costs *and* productivity of
various uses of the environment.

In practice, it will seldom be possible to measure external costs with any degree of precision as a basis for charges. We do not know the full extent of environmental damages from many activities. They are widespread and often occur in small doses that have a measurable impact only after long periods of accumulation. Furthermore, some types of damage are of a type that are not readily quantifiable in dollar terms. For example, there are real costs from the constant noise bombardment in urban areas, but how can one put a dollar value on irritation and discomfort? Because charges based on external costs are thus not feasible, policy formulators have concerned themselves with ways of reaping as much as possible of the benefits of such charges in a more practical system.

Setting Limits to the Use of Environmental Resources

A more workable system of setting charges starts with the familiar concept of ambient standards. Some of the important advantages of charges in the theoretical model carry over to this alternative. The goal of this approach is the achievement of a preset, specified level of ambient quality.

Ambient standards can be set for an appropriate region by a combination of analytical procedures and political processes. Technical experts identify, to the extent possible, the consequences of different levels of ambient quality, for example, the likelihood that certain types of fish will survive at different levels of dissolved oxygen, and to the extent possible, estimate the costs of attaining those levels. The choice of the target level of dissolved oxygen is then made in the political-administrative process. In essence, the public decides "on admittedly incomplete data" how much clean air, water, or quiet it is willing to buy.

Ambient standards, at least for air and water quality, are a long-standing part of the environmental management program in this country. The Clean Air Act and the Federal Water Pollution Control Act mandate the establishment of such standards. National air quality standards and water quality standards for virtually all

of the river basins and airsheds of the country have been developed using the process described above or elements thereof.[5]

The following discussion focuses on a uniform charge for a given region—a water pollution charge that is the same for all sources of a pollutant in a given river basin or water quality control area. This is not the only charge configuration that is possible. The charge on a biodegradable substance could vary according to the location of a source, for example. However, such schemes complicate our explanation of charges and in practice might pose administrative problems that would outweigh their advantages.[6]

In theory there exists a price on environmentally harmful behavior that will result in attainment of any given ambient quality standard. Individual sources would respond to such a charge just as they would to the theoretically ideal type of charge. As discussed earlier, charges on the dumping of any kind of waste into the environment will cause rational cost-minimizing individual sources to reduce their discharges to the point at which the cost of the next incremental unit of discharge reduction equals the charge. To the extent that control costs vary from source to source, the level of control will vary from source to source. However, if the correct charge is imposed, the cumulative effect of these individual cost-minimizing decisions will be a reduction in total discharges sufficient to achieve the desired ambient level of air or water quality.

This type of charge will not result in an optimal market equilibrium (unless by pure coincidence). The price that polluters pay may be more or less than the external costs that their polluting discharges create. The charge will work to bring about the level of air or water quality that is politically chosen. Setting the correct charge level to accomplish this is not a simple task, but unlike the task of identifying all external costs of pollution, it can be accom-

---

[5] A particularly thorough and well-documented example is the establishment of water quality standards in the Delaware River Estuary. See Allen V. Kneese and Blair T. Bower, *Managing Water Quality: Economics, Technology, and Institutions* (Baltimore, Johns Hopkins University Press for Resources for the Future, 1968).

[6] Some of the elements of a geographically variable charge scheme are discussed in Kneese and Bower, *Managing Water Quality.*

plished given the necessary data and analytic tools, as discussed below.

A charge approach centered on ambient quality retains a number of the beneficial features of the charge approach based on environmental damages. Both have the effect, solely through the economic incentive they provide, of concentrating discharge reductions where they are the least costly. Since the price is the same for all dischargers of a given waste, or residual, in a given area, they will all control to the same marginal cost level, the marginal cost of an item being the extra cost involved in producing an extra unit of that item. This does not mean that they will control to the same discharge level (e.g., 80 percent reduction). Marginal costs for a given range of control often vary substantially from one type of source to another. Those polluters for whom control is relatively expensive will eliminate a smaller percentage of their discharges than those for whom control is relatively inexpensive. For instance, a charge might cause factory A, with high control costs, to eliminate 70 percent of its waste discharge while factory B, with lower costs, would eliminate 90 percent of its waste flow. The charge scheme takes advantage of the difference in control costs among sources to keep total control costs down.

Notice that the charges approach will result in lower total costs than one which seeks to attain the same level of ambient quality by requiring A and B to reduce their discharges to the same level, say 85 percent. In the above example, the cost to factory A of controlling each unit between 70 percent and 85 percent reduction would be greater than the amount saved by factory B in not controlling each unit from 90 percent down to 85 percent reduction. Factory B's marginal costs are lower than the charge for every unit of control below 90 percent (or else it would not have been profitable to control that much), while factory A's marginal costs are higher than the charge for every unit above 70 percent (or else it would have been profitable to control more). This comparison is particularly important, because the present regulatory approach to air and water pollution control calls for uniform effluent standards within various categories and subcategories of sources. This will result in higher total control costs for each category or subcategory than would a charge system.

The cost effectiveness of the charges approach has been illustrated in model analyses of the costs of achieving a given level of water quality in the Delaware Estuary using alternative strategies, including an effluent charge and uniform control.[7] This study made use of a mathematical model of the estuary and waste reduction costs for different types of sources to assess total control costs. The charge approach was projected to result in substantially lower control costs (about 50 percent lower) than the uniform reduction approach.

Other major benefits of the charges approach were discussed in chapter 1. Briefly, a charge presents a person or firm engaged in an environmentally damaging activity with an immediate incentive to control it. The activity itself creates a financial liability that cannot be avoided by delaying payment or putting off adopting control measures. The source can legally reduce that liability only by taking steps to reduce the discharge.[8] There is no delay pending completion of enforcement actions before there is an economic incentive to cut back the polluting activity. In addition, the charges approach leaves the question of control techniques and technology to the discharger. For instance, each pollutant discharger faced with a charge on discharges of a given substance can adopt any measure it chooses to reduce those discharges. It can treat the wastes or adopt process or input changes that generate less waste in the first place. Furthermore, because the discharger still pays a charge on the part of its discharge that is not controlled, it has an incentive to continue to search for innovative control measures that will lower its marginal control costs and enable it to save more money.[9] This is an improvement over the regulatory approach, which is somewhat biased toward waste treatment, an option that is often more expensive than alternative cleanup measures.

[7] See Kneese and Bower, *Managing Water Quality*, pp. 158–164.

[8] The source can also reduce the charge liability by hiding the activity from the administering agency. The whole question of measuring pollutant discharges, which is very important in this as well as other pollution control strategies, is discussed in a later chapter on monitoring.

[9] Some charge proposals would do away with all or part of the charge on the uncontrolled discharge so long as prescribed effluent or ambient standards were met. See chapter 3, which presents various practical applications of the charge idea.

Setting the Charge

We now return to the question of how a regulatory agency can determine the charge level that will cause various sources of a given pollutant in a region to reduce their discharges so that the combined effect is achievement of the desired ambient quality goal.

One way to set the charge would be by trial and error. It would be possible just to set a charge, observe its effect, and then move it up or down as indicated until the ambient quality reached and held the desired level. Such an approach has the advantage of administrative simplicity.

The trial-and-error method, however, has several major drawbacks that preclude its adoption. First, if the initial charge was well off the mark, some, perhaps all, of the control cost savings associated with charges might be lost. The trial charge could induce dischargers to make decisions (for instance, to install a treatment plant of a certain size) that could not be changed without substantial additional cost if the charge were changed to an extent that made a different level of control economically rational. Furthermore, the process of deciding on a pollution control strategy and implementing the decision can take several years. The trial-and-error method could result in a long period of oscillation before the ambient quality standard was finally met.

While a crude trial-and-error approach will not work, it is not necessarily difficult to adjust the charge level within a relatively narrow range. Most sources can adjust their control levels to a limited degree without a substantial change in cost. This is because, for a given control strategy, a range of control is possible with a given level of capital investment. Thus, a firm that has installed an expensive treatment system in response to some charge level will probably not need to scrap that system to increase its control level if the charge is raised by a small amount. Furthermore, it is possible for sources to build a limited degree of flexibility into their control approaches if they know that the charge is subject to minor adjustments. It is not, however, possible to plan effectively for major alterations in charge levels.

It is theoretically feasible to set an acceptably accurate charge, at least in the areas of air and water pollution. Estimated average

marginal cost data for different types of sources can be used to estimate the effect of different charge levels on the discharges from
different sources in an area. Mathematical models of river basins
or air pollution regions can be used to estimate the impact on
ambient quality of various discharge levels at different sources in
the area. With these two procedures, it is possible to come reasonably close to the desired charge level.[10]

The needed cost data are not an insuperable obstacle. Estimated
average data for different classes of dischargers are all that is
needed. This is much more practical for an agency to obtain than
specific data about each discharger's costs, which would be required to properly implement the least-cost effluent standards approach. In addition, the data needs for a charge system are not
likely to be greater than those of the present standards approach.
In setting effluent standards under the Federal Water Pollution
Control Act Amendments of 1972, for instance, EPA must estimate
control costs for various industry and subindustry groups, and in
addition obtain financial and other data to determine the economic
impact of proposed standards. Some usable estimated average marginal control cost data needed for setting charges are available or
can be relatively easily obtained from existing data. The methodology for estimating industry control costs where they are not now
available is reasonably well developed. It would be a major task to
obtain enough data for a nationwide program, but not an impossible one, particularly if the system were limited to one or two key
measures of pollution.

Mathematical models are needed because ambient quality is not
just a function of the amount of pollutant discharged. Ambient concentrations are a result of the amount and pattern of wastes discharged and of natural phenomena related to the dispersion and
transformation of materials in the environment. For example, the
level of dissolved oxygen in a stream is a complex function of discharges and such parameters as streamflow, turbulence, and tem-

[10] For a more detailed description of this process, see Phillip D. Reed, "The Use
of Economic Disincentives in Environmental Quality Management," a paper prepared at the Environmental Law Institute for the National Academy of Sciences,
July 1, 1976; and Clifford S. Russell, *Residuals Management in Industry* (Baltimore,
Johns Hopkins University Press for Resources for the Future, 1973).

perature—the last affecting both the rate of biological activity bearing upon dissolved oxygen and the ability of the water to dissolve gases. The mathematical formulations relating multiple sources of discharge to ambient conditions are known as transfer functions.

Transfer functions embodied in quantitative waste reduction cost models make it possible to experiment with different waste reduction strategies for attaining ambient standards. Such models can be used in conjunction with the estimated average marginal cost data to test the likely effect of different charge levels. It would be a major task to develop models for enough areas to implement a charge system on a large scale. The modeling techniques, while not without some flaws, have been the subject of substantial experimentation and development, particularly with respect to water.[11] To apply them on a nationwide or even statewide basis would be no small undertaking. However, it should be noted that no system of environmental management based on ambient quality—including the present regulatory approach—can function properly without appropriate models. Each system must have a reasonably accurate means of relating changes in discharge levels and locations to changes in ambient quality. With models to provide this information and estimated average marginal control cost data, the initial charge level set by a regulatory agency can be an informed, reasonably accurate decision and not a shot in the dark.

Concluding Comment

In this chapter we have laid out the bare bones of an economic rationale for a charge system to reduce pollution. Such a rationale provides insights for understanding the root causes of the problem of environmental degradation and points toward attractive approaches to its solution. But the formulation is, after all, very ab-

[11] See, for instance, Kneese and Bower, *Managing Water Quality*; Russell, *Residuals Management*; and Bruce Ackerman, Susan Rose Ackerman, James W. Sawyer, Jr., and Dale Henderson, *The Uncertain Search for Environmental Quality* (New York, Free Press, 1974.)

stract. A host of technical, legal, behavioral, and political problems and issues arise in making operational the policies this rationale suggests. Moreover, economic theory has relatively little to say about such major issues as equity and effectiveness. These are taken up in chapter 6. We are obliged to turn now to the complex issues of implementation.

3

A Survey of Charges Applications

Introduction

Dozens of environmental quality management schemes that employ the charges concept to a significant degree have been refined into detailed proposals or put into practice. In this chapter we survey the results of these efforts to design and implement such programs.

In this discussion of charges applications, we try to cover the field, and if necessary sometimes sacrifice detail for comprehensiveness. The chapter covers charges as applied to air and water pollution, solid wastes, land use, noise, congestion, energy conservation, and hazardous substances. We describe how important implementation questions are answered in each program and proposal discussed, but do not attempt to describe the schemes in complete detail or to analyze them in depth. Others have conducted more thorough studies of a number of the charges systems discussed here. We include references to these studies for readers interested in looking into particular schemes or approaches in greater detail. Our purpose here is to provide a catalog of programs and proposals that demonstrates the wide applicability of the charges approach and highlights a limited number of key implementation considerations.

To the extent possible with available information, the descriptions of specific charges schemes focus on seven basic issues. They are:

What is the purpose or goal of the charges system?

What economic variables provide the basis for computing the charge rate?

To what extent does the charge rate vary with environmental and economic factors?

What specific activities are charged?

What is done to make the charge system administratively workable?

How are the charge revenues used?

How does the charge system interact with standards systems addressing the same environmental problem?

Purpose

One of the first things to consider in reviewing a charges system is the goal that the system is designed to achieve. The system's purpose determines its structure to a significant degree and, conversely, practical constraints on the system's structure can determine what goals can be achieved with it.

The theoretically ideal charges systems discussed in chapter 2 had the far-reaching purpose of internalizing pollution externalities and thus achieving an efficient market allocation of environmental resources. For practical reasons spelled out in chapter 2, this approach will not work. The charges schemes reviewed here have less ambitious goals.

One alternative purpose is to achieve specific environmental goals by creating economic incentives for individual polluters to control their environmentally damaging activities. Sometimes such a charge system is designed to achieve an ambient quality standard. Thus, the proposed water pollution charge discussed in chapter 2 as an alternative to the theoretically pure charge is intended to achieve ambient water quality standards as the cumulative result of charge-induced effluent cutbacks by individual sources. Other systems are designed to induce dischargers to achieve standards or to institute specific control measures. For instance, Hungary levies charges on all those who discharge water pollutants in excess of effluent standards to induce them to comply with the standards.

Another very different purpose of charges is the generation of revenue to combat pollution or its effects. Some revenue-oriented

charges are intended to finance public or collective control measures. The water pollution charges system of West Germany's Ruhr river basin is the classic example of this approach. Other systems are designed to provide money to protect people from pollution that reaches the environment. Japan's airport noise charge, designed to pay for soundproofing homes near airports and similar measures, is of this type. A third type of revenue-oriented charge is intended to provide funds to compensate pollution victims. It is exemplified by Japan's landmark compensation law.

In practice, charge systems seldom are limited to a single purpose. All three types of revenue-oriented charges could cause polluters to control their pollution, and this is often an important secondary goal in such systems. The generation of revenue to finance environmental protection activities is often a secondary goal of charges schemes whose primary objective is curtailing the environmentally damaging activities of individual sources. Moreover, some charge schemes seem to give equal weight to several objectives.

Economic Basis of the Charge Rate

If a charges system is to be effective in achieving its purpose, the charge rate must be based on the proper economic variable. This rather simple point is fundamental to the proper design of charges systems. Elsewhere we have discussed the fact that charges intended to fully internalize the external costs of pollution must take those costs into account. We have also shown how a charge designed to create an incentive for increased pollution control by individual sources (whether to achieve ambient quality standards or discharge standards) must be based on the costs to those particular sources of achieving the necessary levels of control. The focus on pollution control costs is dictated by the fact that each source looks to its own costs in deciding what level of control to adopt in response to a charge. It is also obvious that the rate of charges intended to finance public measures to control pollution discharges or reduce their impact should be based on the costs of the particular measures in question. Those costs determine how much revenue will be needed and therefore how high the charge rate should be set.

Thus, the economic variable that is the basis of the charge rate determines the nature of the system's impact.

The need to base charge rates on certain economic variables creates constraints for those wishing to implement the charges. It is not always possible or practical to obtain necessary data on the critical variable. As discussed in chapter 2, the lack of adequate data on the full external costs of pollution is the Achilles heel of the theoretically ideal charges system. Pollution control cost data, on the other hand, are more readily available, so charges designed to bring about desired levels of pollution control are often more practical. In any specific charge scheme of this type, there are still important choices to be made, however. Are typical or average pollution control costs for an industry adequate or is it necessary to dig deeper and get cost data for subcategories or individual sources? Should average or marginal costs be used? Issues of this type are discussed elsewhere in this book. Suffice it to say here that they can significantly affect the impact and the data-gathering costs of a charge system.

Where the purpose of the charge system is to finance specific public or collective activities to control pollution or counter its effects, data problems can be avoided if the nature and cost of the activities to be financed can be spelled out in advance. This is not always easy and can be a key issue in the design of such programs. Wherever possible in our discussion of specific charge systems, we will indicate how each resolved the sometimes difficult problem of finding a practical economic variable on which to base the charge rate.

Charge Rate Variability

Once the goal of the charge system has been identified and a workable economic basis for the charge rate has been selected, a number of detailed design issues must be resolved. First among these is whether the charge rate should be uniform or variable. The economists' theoretically ideal charge would be highly sensitive to changes in the many variables that affect the level of damages caused by the charged activity. The flexibility of such a pricing system is not practical where prices (charges) are to be determined by a central authority rather than a decentralized market mech-

anism. Nevertheless, the question of variable versus uniform charges is important in centralized systems as well and is discussed in detail in chapter 6. Uniform charges are attractive because they are easier to set and administer. They are also simpler and therefore easier for legislators and the public to understand. On the other hand, variable charges can serve several useful functions. Where the purpose is inducing sources to achieve pollution control objectives, the objectives can be met at lower cost if the charge varies with the assimilative capacity of the particular environmental system involved or with the pollution control costs of the specific sources involved. Where the purpose is financing public pollution control or impact reduction measures, variable charges can allocate the financial burdens among different sources on a more equitable basis.

As we shall see, the question of uniform versus variable charges has been answered in a number of different ways in actual charges programs and in proposed systems. There are uniform charges such as the noise charge on jet airplane landings, proposed by the Organisation for Economic Co-operation and Development. The charge rate would be the same whatever type of plane is involved and regardless of the overall level of noise prevailing at the time of the landing. Other charges can vary by region, such as France's water pollution charges. A third group of charges would vary with the time of day to take account of changes in the assimilative capacity of the environmental system. Proposed automobile congestion charges for the Los Angeles basin are of this type.

The Activity Charged

Ideally, charges should be levied directly on the activity to be influenced. In economic theory, a charge designed to correct an externality should be levied directly on the externality itself. For instance, emissions of sulfur oxides are the externalities of many fuel-burning operations. The ideal charge would be applied to the emissions themselves. Even where the charge has the more modest purpose of inducing adherence to prescribed pollution reduction levels, it will be most effective, all other things being equal, if levied directly on the pollution itself.

It is not always possible, however, to levy charges at the optimal point in an externality-generating process. Political, technical, and administrative obstacles may effectively block access to that point. Thus, designers of charges systems must often choose less than ideal targets for the charges because of practical considerations.

A charge designed to control automobile emissions is a useful example of how these issues affect implementation. If the charge were levied directly on emissions, drivers would have a clear incentive to cut emissions and would have numerous ways of doing so: driving less, purchasing cleaner cars, and operating and maintaining their cars so as to minimize emissions. The charge would send constructive economic shock waves in various directions. Consumers would demand cars that generate low levels of pollution and services that keep them operating cleanly. They would also demand improved alternative modes of transportation that generate less pollution. Contrast this with the effect of a charge on auto manufacturers based on the emissions from their new cars. The incentives to cut driving and properly maintain pollution control systems would be lost (although the charge could be set up to encourage manufacturers to build cars whose pollution control systems needed little maintenance). Thus, the point at which the pollution itself is generated is the ideal target for a charge.

There are serious practical problems with such a charge, however. Charges levied directly on auto emissions require regular monitoring of emissions from millions of autos. It appears that reliable technology for such monitoring is not available, that the administrative requirements would be very heavy, and that both monitoring and collection of the charges would cause crippling political opposition from one of the broadest interest groups in our society. In such cases, it may be necessary to settle for a less effective solution and charge automobile manufacturers.

In some cases the effectiveness of a charge on a less than optimal early stage of a polluting process can be enhanced by other measures. (Economic theorists have argued that a combination of charges and subsidies on all inputs and outputs of a polluting activity could achieve the same result as a charge on the externality itself.) A practical example might be a subsidy to encourage motorists to have their cars serviced regularly, paid out of the revenue from the charge on auto manufacturers. The charge on manufac-

turers could be set up so as to encourage the production of cars whose pollution control systems needed little maintenance. The existing charges programs and proposals discussed in the following sections illustrate many different resolutions of the problems of finding an effective and workable point of impact for the charge.

Administration

One of the most important issues in implementing charges (or any other environmental quality management system) is the administrative feasibility of the approach taken. In chapters 4 and 6 we address major administrative tasks, such as charge setting, monitoring, and charge collection. In this chapter we have mentioned administrative constraints affecting the proper basis for the charge rate, the stage at which to levy the charge, and other implementation issues. We need not spell out again the important administrative questions. In our discussion of charge programs and proposals, however, we do give separate attention to key administrative issues because they are often the pivotal questions facing designers of charges systems.

Use of Revenues

One of the most ticklish questions to address in putting charges into practice is what to do with the revenue they provide. There are many constructive uses for the funds. As we have seen, some charges schemes are implemented primarily to finance public programs of pollution control, pollution impact reduction, or to compensate victims of pollution damages. Even where the charge scheme has a different primary purpose, the money can be applied in ways that increase the program's effectiveness or its political acceptability. However, as chapter 6 indicates, there is also a grave danger of "revenue addiction," that is, that the purposes of the charge system will be perverted by institutions or people that receive the revenues and seek to maximize their income at the expense of the original goals of the system. In our discussion of charges programs and proposals we indicate what is done or would be done with the revenues. For instance, the short-lived New York recycling incentive tax (solid waste) on plastic containers skirted

the revenue addiction problem by funneling the money into general government revenues. Other systems, for instance the product disposal (solid waste) charges in legislation suggested by Senator Gary Hart, would target the money for program purposes, in this case administering the program, paying recycling subsidies, and providing municipalities with money for solid waste disposal programs.

Charges and Standards

Charges and standards can be mutually supportive approaches to environmental quality management. There are many ways in which the two approaches can be used in tandem. In some cases one approach will not work without help from the other. In applying charges systems to environmental problems, it is thus necessary to consider whether and how standards should be worked into the scheme. The proper resolution of this question in any given case will require careful consideration of a variety of issues. In our review of programs and proposals, most of which combine charges and standards in some fashion, we look into how each resolves these issues.

Charge designers must consider the fact that charges alone will not always be effective. We have indicated elsewhere how a charge system can be used to achieve ambient quality standards. However, effluent or emission standards may also be necessary adjuncts to charges in other situations. Some polluters with market power might pass the charges along to their customers rather than adopt pollution control measures. Minimum discharge control standards would counter such problems if they arose. Events such as treatment plant breakdowns could disrupt the normal economics of control to the point that it would be cheaper to pay the charge than to adopt alternative controls (shutdown or hauling wastes elsewhere for treatment). Locally serious pulse discharges could result. Maximum daily discharge limits could counteract such temporary lapses in the effectiveness of charges. Where there is no margin for error as to the amount of a given pollutant that enters the environment, for instance, with certain toxic substances, charges alone probably provide inadequate control. Standards governing production, handling, and disposal of toxics may be necessary.

Where emission or effluent standards programs are already in place and a changeover to charges is warranted, charges and standards may have to coexist. Rapid transitions to major charges systems are probably not feasible and could cause environmental protection efforts to lose what ground they have gained while administrators and regulatees become accustomed to the requirements of the new approach and the bugs are worked out of the charges mechanism. Thus, the limitations of charges must be taken into account in putting them into effect.

Regulatory schemes based on emissions or effluent standards also have limitations and charges can help overcome them. Where technology for controlling a particular pollution problem is lacking, strict standards can force development of the technology. However, the process can be dragged out over long periods of time because the technological debates tie up permit negotiations and administrative and judicial enforcement actions. Charges could relieve this problem by providing an immediate incentive for sources to develop new control technology where necessary. Standards-based regulatory systems have had enforcement problems even where acceptable control technology exists. The high cost of and very low return from pollution control gives discharge sources, particularly those in weak financial shape, a powerful incentive to put off compliance with the control requirements dictated by standards. Traditional enforcement measures ignore this economic disincentive and are either too mild to counteract it (e.g., administrative orders) or too severe to be readily invoked (massive fines, jail sentences, factory shutdowns). Charges on discharges in excess of discharge levels allowed by standards or fees for violating specific control requirements can, if based on the costs of compliance with the standards or requirements, make enforcement efforts much more effective.

In conclusion, the application of charges to practical problems of environmental protection requires consideration of a variety of issues and recognition of a number of constraints. What can be achieved with a charge? Practical matters like the lack of good data on environmental damages and the existence of partially effective major standards-based regulatory programs in some areas place limits on the goals that can reasonably be pursued. Even so, charges can serve a variety of functions, from helping to enforce

emission or effluent limitations or supplementing the abatement incentives created by standards, to independently inducing achievement of specific environmental quality goals. What must be considered in designing a charge system? At least seven basic issues warrant consideration. In sum, the charge must be targeted and structured carefully to ensure that it will have the desired effect without consuming too many administrative resources or creating dysfunctional secondary incentives. Having identified the constraints and key issues relating to the practical application of charges, we now turn our attention to examples of such application.

Air Pollution

The charges approach has received a great deal of attention as a response to various air pollution problems. East Germany has instituted a program of emission charges on a wide range of air pollutants. On a broader front, Japan has established a system of air (and water) pollution charges for both stationary and moving sources to compensate victims of pollution-related diseases. Connecticut has instituted a system of economics-based administrative civil penalties for violating air emission standards and corrective orders. Similar proposals have been included in recent revisions of the Federal Clean Air Act. While these penalty schemes are definitely not emission charges, nevertheless, like some emission charges, the penalties are designed to make it economically rational for sources to control their emissions to desired levels.

Charge systems have been proposed to combat air pollution from automobiles by encouraging the development and purchase of cars or fuels that generate relatively low levels of polluting emissions. One such approach places a tax on the lead content of gasoline. A second would tax new vehicles on the basis of their emissions. A tax on retail sales of gasoline based on each car's emission level has also been proposed. Finally, a number of charge schemes aimed at other automobile-caused environmental problems have been proposed to help fight emissions. Among these are gasoline taxes, which are discussed in the section on energy, and road use charges, which are discussed in the congestion section.

East German Air Emission Charges

In 1973, East Germany established an ambitious program that levies charges on emissions of 113 different air pollutants.[1] The charges are paid by every source whose emissions of a charged pollutant exceed the national emission standard for that substance. The incentive effect of the charges is intensified by a prohibition against passing charge costs along to customers through increased prices. The revenues generated by the charges are kept in the region in which they are paid and are used for air pollution control planning, environmental improvement, and compensation for those injured by air pollution.

Japan's Compensation Law

In 1973 Japan enacted the Law for the Compensation of Pollution-Related Health Damage.[2] The law sets up a system of environmental charges designed to finance the payment of compensation to individuals who suffer health damage as a result of air or water pollution. The compensation law is discussed in this section, but could just as easily be included in the sections on water pollution or hazardous and toxic substances.

The goal of the law is to compensate the victims of diseases and other physical ailments caused by pollution. The charge levied on a discharger is based on certain health costs arising from the pollution for which that discharger is responsible. Determining the appropriate charge is difficult, because the effects of different types of pollution on health and the causal links between a given discharge and an identified health effect are not fully understood. In order to avoid this problem, the Japanese compensation program establishes a variety of presumptions that allow administrative "proof" of entitlement without wrestling with difficult questions

---

[1] Peter H. Sand, "The Socialist Response: Environmental Protection Law in the Socialist Democratic Republic," *Ecology Law Quarterly* vol. 3, no. 3 (Summer 1973) pp. 451–490.

[2] Julian Gresser, "The Japanese Act for the Compensation of Pollution-Related Health Damage: An Introductory Assessment," *Environmental Law Review* vol. 5 (December 1975) p. 50229; Julian Gresser, Akio Morishima, Koichiro Fujikura, "The Law for the Compensation of Pollution-Related Disease: An Assessment of the First Two Years of Implementation," Interim report (undated).

of direct causation on a case-by-case basis. In carrying out the plan, the Japanese use statistics and epidemiology to allocate social responsibility for injuries in a fashion that is the most advanced application of these tools by any nation. The following discussion of the procedure is simplified, but touches on the main points.

First, toxic substances that could be shown to be statistically correlated with specific identifiable health problems were designated. Among them were sulfur oxides, which have been linked to respiratory ailments. Next, pollution zones were identified, on the basis of extensive investigations of concentrations of the designated pollutants and high incidences of the specified diseases.

If it is determined that apparent victims have the designated disease and were present long enough in a specific pollution zone to infer that pollution caused the disease, they are entitled to compensation for medical care, rehabilitation, disability, survivors' benefits, and funeral expenses. There is no payment for pain and suffering or property damage. Compensation for the designated costs is paid out of revenues from charges on polluters. The same charge funds pay for half the cost of medical and rehabilitation facilities required by pollution victims, but not for the administration of the law.

The charges levied under the compensation act are calculated so as to allocate the costs of compensating pollution victims among polluters on one of two bases. The first category of charges is applicable to sulfur oxides and other multisource pollution problems. In setting charges for sulfur oxides, the total costs to be paid are estimated using data on the population in pollution zones and the incidence of compensable respiratory problems. Twenty percent of this figure is allocated to automobiles (and paid out of a preexisting yearly automobile tax based on car weight). The remaining 80 percent of the costs are allocated among all sources of airborne sulfur oxides, whether or not they are located in a designated pollution zone. However, those in the zone pay at a higher rate than those outside it.

The other category of charges applies to specific dischargers that can be identified as the only source of a particular substance in an area. Such sources pay all the costs of compensating their victims. Charges in this category are thus not related to discharge levels.

There are several points concerning the administration of the compensation law that bear mention here. First, the series of presumptions that makes the system workable also requires the collection and analysis of a great deal of economic, scientific, and medical data. Second, a national industrial association has played a key role in implementing the program. It acted as a spokesman for industry in structuring the program and endorsed the system as finally adopted. The association's continuing acceptance has apparently acted as a powerful disincentive for individual firms to try to evade their responsibilities under the act. As a result, there have been few problems with monitoring or collection.

The compensation law is a supplement to the preexisting pollution control system. It does not supplant the regulatory system, nor does it preclude efforts by compensated victims to obtain additional damages from polluters by bargaining or in court.

The compensation program has been in effect for two years, but there is only a limited amount of information on its impact.[3] Large sums have been paid out for compensation (one steel company has paid over $6 million). While ambient levels of sulfur oxides have declined since the program went into effect, there are other possible explanations for this improvement (e.g., economic recession). There is no evidence yet on the extent to which emission control measures have been adopted as a result of the charges. Since the program went into effect, there has been a trend toward industrial relocation into relatively clean rural areas, but again the causal connection has not been proven. Perhaps the most important consequence of the compensation law is that it has demonstrated that a large-scale charge system designed to internalize some of the more egregious external costs of pollution can be implemented successfully.

The Sulfur Tax

The use of charges to help control emissions from stationary air pollution sources has not been tried in this country. However,

---

[3] Gresser, Morishima, and Fujikura, ibid.

there have been some proposals in the area that deserve mention. The Nixon administration proposed a nationwide sulfur tax in 1970 and again the following year.[4] A similar program was spelled out by the Coalition to Tax Pollution.[5] The proposals received a great deal of attention but were not adopted.[6]

The sulfur taxes were designed to create an immediate and continuing incentive to abate sulfur emissions. The tax levels in both proposals appear to have been based on the same estimates of sulfur oxide control costs and social damages. There was a significant difference in the charge formula which would have been applied under the two schemes. The administration's sulfur tax was to be 15¢ per pound of sulfur (the control cost estimate) in regions which had not attained primary air quality standards, 10¢ per pound where primary (but not secondary) standards were achieved, and zero in regions which had met the secondary standards. The Coalition's tax was to be 20¢ per pound of sulfur (midway between the control cost and social damage estimates) in all areas of the country. The difference is important, because the variable charge would encourage relocation of industries to areas that sur-

---

[4] Material Relating to the Administrative Proposals for Environmental Protection, House Committee on Ways and Means, Print H-782-9 (February 1972). See also William A. Irwin and Richard A. Liroff, *Economic Disincentives for Pollution Control: Legal, Political and Administrative Dimensions*, pp. 127–131. (Prepared for EPA, July 1974, and available from the National Technical Information Service, Springfield, Va.); "The President's 1972 Environmental Program" (Washington, Council on Environmental Quality) p. 44; "The President's 1973 Environmental Program" (Washington, Council on Environmental Quality) p. 20; Edward I. Selig, ed., "Effluent Charges on Air and Water Pollution," Environmental Law Institute, Monograph Series 1, re: Conference, October 1971, published 1973, pp. 52–61.

[5] Irwin and Liroff, *Economic Disincentives*, pp. 131–132 and Selig, "Effluent Charges," pp. 52–61.

[6] Serious interest in the sulfur oxide tax or charge has revived. The Navajo Indian tribe has imposed a sulfur tax on polluters located on their lands. As of March 1977, a proposal for a state sulfur oxide tax was being developed in New Mexico and a draft proposal was under consideration in California. At the same time, several groups were preparing legislative proposals for national sulfur oxide taxes or charges.

The application of sulfur charges in Europe and the United States is given detailed attention in the recently published *Pollution Charges, An Assessment,* Report by the Secretariat, Organisation for Economic Co-operation and Development (Paris, 1976). (Hereafter cited as OECD.)

passed the secondary standards and could lead to significant deterioration of areas with very clean air.

The tax levels under both systems, however, were somewhat arbitrary. Abatement technology for sulfur emissions was in a markedly undeveloped state, and available data on social damages were both limited and of questionable validity. Thus the precise extent to which external costs would have been internalized and sulfur oxide emissions controlled under either charge is open to speculation.

The Coalition's proposal resolved the question of who pays in an interesting fashion. The tax was to be levied on fuel suppliers on the basis of the sulfur content of the fuel sold. Presumably suppliers would then raise their prices. Each subsequent processor or user of the fuel would be paid 20¢ per pound for any sulfur it removed from the fuel. This ensured that there would be a continuing incentive to remove sulfur from the fuel stream at all points in the production and use process before emission into the air. It also avoided the difficult problem of monitoring emissions at numerous sources and put the burden of proving amounts of sulfur removed on users. However, for sources of sulfur emissions that do not burn sulfur-bearing fuels, for example, copper smelters, the dischargers themselves would pay the tax and some emission monitoring would be necessary. The number of such dischargers is small, although in a few areas their contribution to sulfur emissions is quite large.

Excess Emissions Fee

In 1976, the U.S. House of Representatives adopted amendments to the Clean Air Act that established a fee on emissions by major stationary sources in excess of applicable emission limitations.[7] The fees were to be based on the costs of achieving the emission limitations. This illustrates the use of a charge as a means of achieving a regulatory emission standard. However, the excess

7 H.R. 10498, 94 Cong. 1 sess., §105.

emissions fee provision was not included in the amendments approved by the House-Senate conference.

Connecticut Economic Enforcement Measures

The state of Connecticut has recently established a system of civil assessments and sureties that share some important features of the charges approach.[8] In the fall of 1976, the U.S. House and Senate agreed on amendments to the Clean Air Act that would install a related system of civil penalties on the national level (instead of excess emission fees). However, a filibuster prevented enactment of the entire package of amendments before the end of that session of Congress. A similar provision is included in the recently enacted Clean Air Act Amendments of 1977 (section 118). This type of enforcement measure is designed to fill a gap between mild steps, such as toothless administrative orders, and severe ones, such as injunctions entirely shutting down polluters. It shares with many of the charge systems discussed here the characteristic of making environmentally damaging activities economically irrational.

The Connecticut program enables enforcement officers to eliminate the economic advantages that regulated sources now enjoy if they delay or avoid compliance with pollution control requirements. Assessment provisions that have been implemented apply to failure to submit progress reports, violation of emission standards, and violation of the terms of abatement orders.

A special program for violation of requirements for the operation and maintenance (O & M) of abatement equipment has been proposed but not adopted. The O & M program has four major components: (1) permits for sources that violate O & M requirements after notice, (2) standards of performance for control equipment operation, (3) continuous monitoring of emission and/or control equipment operating parameters, and (4) assessments based on the cost savings from failure to properly operate and maintain control equipment.[9]

[8] Connecticut Enforcement Project, *Economic Law Enforcement* vol. II, *Strengthening Environmental Law Enforcement: Air Pollution* (Washington, EPA, 1975).

[9] Connecticut Enforcement Project Final Report, vol. V, pp. 1–15.

The assessment (or surety) taxes away the economic value of not complying with control requirements. For example, when a source delays taking steps to abate emissions that exceed state standards, the source could be required either to post a surety or to pay a civil assessment. In either case, the amount is calculated with a commonly used businessman's capital budgeting formula that takes into account all the installed capital and operating costs saved, the effect of taxes and inflation, and the rate of return that could be obtained by investing the money saved in a profitable venture.

In Connecticut, the economic enforcement devices are applied selectively to sources that have violated emission standards and abatement requirements and have not responded to milder enforcement measures. In this respect these assessments are significantly different from charges. Assessments are paid only by the recalcitrant few, while charges are paid by all dischargers. For most Connecticut dischargers, it is the threat of civil penalties that creates the economic incentive to comply. The provisions included in the federal Clean Air Act allow somewhat less discretion in requiring payments. They assess penalties automatically for a large class of sources that are in violation of emission limitations and other requirements.

The Connecticut assessments are levied administratively in accordance with procedures designed to avoid several roadblocks. The state need not go to court to collect a penalty. The potentially overwhelming task of calculating the costs of compliance for a variety of different types of sources is simplified. Initially, penalties are based on estimates which are often derived from simple curves relating abatement costs to readily measurable variables. The penalty amounts can be corrected later, when actual abatement cost data are available. The procedures for levying the penalties provide hearings and court appeals to protect the rights of sources, but discourage frivolous delays because the penalties continue to add up while the appeals are being taken. The Connecticut system collects penalties efficiently through court orders that are issued by court clerks *without judicial action* and that are enforceable by the sheriff, just as court judgments are collected from those who refuse to pay. Revenues are likely to be small and

sporadic, since effective penalties will deter violations. They are funnelled into general revenues.

The Connecticut program is still in its infancy. The first major penalty has been levied and an administrative hearing and probable court appeal are pending. However, warning letters notifying violators of potential civil penalty liability have cut abatement delays by 30 to 40 percent, minor penalties for failure to submit progress reports have increased the submission rate from approximately 50 percent to 98 percent, and sureties required of a few chronic abatement deadline violators have caused a dramatic shift to punctuality. The clear implication is that polluters will respond to measures that make compliance good business.

New Car Emission Taxes and Smog Taxes

There have been several notable attempts to apply the charges to the problems of controlling emissions from motor vehicles. With one relatively limited exception, these programs have not gone beyond the proposal stage. They are discussed here because the proposals have been carefully studied and because the present regulatory approach to auto emission controls has repeatedly run into serious snags.

Two basically different approaches are embodied in proposals for new car emission taxes[10] and smog taxes.[11] The new car tax, often associated with Donald Dewees, is designed to internalize the social costs of auto emissions and thereby to create incentives for manufacturers to build and for consumers to buy cars that generate less pollution. The smog tax would create similar incentives, but is primarily designed to discourage driving and to encourage operation and maintenance of cars with installed pollution control devices so as to minimize emissions. Thus, the two approaches might be most effective if used in tandem.

The new car tax is based on the external costs of vehicular emissions and was to be calculated in several steps. The social costs of auto pollution were to be estimated and divided among dif-

[10] Donald N. Dewees, *Economics and Public Policy: The Auto Pollution Case* (Cambridge, Mass., MIT Press, 1974).

[11] *Hearings on Tax Recommendations of the President Before the Committee on House Ways and Means*, 91 Cong. 2 sess., pt. 1, pp. 369–379 (1970).

ferent types of vehicles, based on estimates of their relative lifelong emissions of various pollutants. The emissions data were to be obtained from tests on production models of every type of vehicle. Cars that met the (original) 1975 emissions standards were to be exempted from the tax.

The smog tax was to be calculated differently. The tax paid for each vehicle was to be based on the costs of keeping emissions down and was to vary from car to car on the basis of results of periodic emission tests. The tax would financially benefit an owner who kept his car and its emission control system functioning efficiently.

The new car emission tax would be of limited effectiveness, because it would affect only one facet of the auto emission problem. It would be paid only on purchase of the car, and would generate no incentive to operate and maintain cars so as to cut down on emissions. Furthermore, there is no assurance that the new car tax would have been large enough to create an effective incentive to build cleaner cars, because it was based on external costs, not emission control costs. On the other hand, such a tax would create an incentive for Detroit to produce, and consumers to purchase, cars that produced low emissions when new, particularly because it would be extracted in one relatively large, highly visible lump that would significantly affect the purchase price of "dirty" cars.

The smog tax would affect the design and purchase of cars and the operation and maintenance of them as well. Demand for low emission cars would be stimulated, because such cars would help keep gas costs down. It is unlikely that this incentive would be as powerful as the new car tax which directly raises purchase prices, however. On the other hand, the smog tax would raise the price of gas for all drivers, thus discouraging driving somewhat. It would also encourage drivers to maintain their cars so as to score well on emissions tests. Since there is evidence that proper maintenance is critical in reducing emissions from older cars, this latter incentive would be very important.

The new car emission charge appears to be relatively easy to administer. The main task would be setting the charge, primarily by testing new car emission levels (assuming existing social cost data could be used). Because the charge would be levied upon sale of the car, and might be collected through the sales tax mech-

anism, monitoring, collection, and enforcement should not present major problems.

The smog tax would involve more difficult administrative requirements. The added burden of testing every vehicle on the road regularly (instead of one of each type of vehicle produced each year) would be significant. There might be enforcement problems stemming from shoddy reporting or falsification of test results. In addition, collection would involve thousands of gasoline retailers who would have to either charge variable rates to reflect different emission ratings, or charge fixed initial rates and grant variable refunds. Both options involve heavy administrative burdens.[12]

Lead Additive Tax

Lead in gasoline is an environmental problem largely because leaded gasoline prevents catalytic converters from operating properly. Since these converters are Detroit's primary means of meeting EPA's auto emission standards, leaded gas could be a major problem. The Nixon administration proposed a lead additive tax in 1970, but Congress rejected the proposal.[13] The New York City scheme, involving a tax of 1¢ per gallon, was adopted several years later and is still in effect.[14]

These schemes were designed to set the stage for regulatory provisions requiring the use of low-lead fuels in cars. By reducing or eliminating the price differential between the fuels, the taxes would increase consumer demand for low-lead fuels. Furthermore,

[12] Another, more limited economic approach to auto pollution is represented by a number of proposals to use existing civil penalties on manufacturers of noncomplying vehicles provided in section 205 of the Clean Air Act. The proposals call for EPA to seek penalties, not at the maximum rate of $10,000 per vehicle, but at rates reflecting the costs of noncompliance with the specific standards in question. These proposals represent a very small step in the direction of charges since the penalties are judicially imposed and therefore would be used in only a limited number of cases. [Taken from W. Andrew Baldwin, "Book Review," *Ecology Law Quarterly* vol. 5, no. 1 (1975) pp. 219–220 and Roger Strelow, "A Solution for Auto Pollution," Point of View Column, *The Washington Post*, Sunday, January 2, 1977, p. C-8.]

[13] *Hearings on Tax Recommendations of the President Before the Committee on House Ways and Means*, 91 Cong. 2 sess., pt. 1, pp. 11–13 (1970). See also, Selig, "Effluent Charges," pp. 75–78.

[14] Telephone interview with Dan Alberga, associate excise tax examiner, New York State Dept. of Taxation and Finances, Commodities Tax Section, December 9, 1976 and "Taxing Leaded Gasoline," McKinsey & Co., Inc., June 1971.

they give producers an incentive to shift over to low-lead gas production without requiring them to undertake all the heavy costs of such a shift at once.

This illustrates an important use of charges as a means of smoothing out transition problems when regulatory programs seek to induce major shifts in production and consumption of a basic commodity.

Water Pollution

Environmental charges have had perhaps their longest history and most widespread use in the area of water pollution control. The charges approach, or elements of it, have been applied to water pollution problems in a host of proposals and programs in the United States and Europe.[15] These systems can be separated into three loosely defined categories. Several water pollution control systems feature effluent charges intended to cause sources to reduce their discharges enough so that legislatively set water quality goals would be achieved. The dominant feature of a second group of charge programs is the use of charge revenues to finance regional or local action to achieve regional water quality standards or other goals. A third set of proposals and programs applies charges in conjunction with effluent standards or similar requirements.

Effluent Charges Oriented to Water Quality

The charge systems in this category share the fact that they seek to induce individual sources to take pollution control steps, the overall result of which will be attainment of prescribed water quality goals. Czechoslovakia provides the sole working example of this approach, but several schemes proposed for use in the United States fall into the same category.

[15] For a recent assessment of charges and water pollution control in Europe, see Ralph W. Johnson and Gardner M. Brown, Jr., *Cleaning up Europe's Waters: Economics, Management and Policies* (New York, Praeger, 1976). An equally recent, though more general look at issues relating to water pollution charges is taken in OECD, *Pollution Charges*.

Czechoslovakia[16] has been using effluent charges to maintain water quality at predetermined levels for the past ten years. A basic charge (referred to as an indemnity) is placed on biological oxygen demand (BOD) and suspended solids (SS). A surtax of from 10 to 100 percent of the basic charge is added, depending on the extent to which the discharge increases the concentration of BOD or SS in the receiving waters. There is apparently also provision for raising the basic rates in basins where the water quality standards are not achieved.

The incentive effect of the Czech charge scheme seems to be directed primarily to inducing proper operation of treatment facilities. Charge amounts are based on the operating costs of available treatment systems. The charges do not reflect capital costs of pollution control treatment and thus would be too low to induce investments in treatment systems or process changes. However, the Czech system takes account of this by allocating charge revenues to subsidies for such investments.

Several features facilitate administration of the Czech charge program. The system appears to be designed to identify the charge levels that will result in desired levels of water quality with some measure of trial and error rather than elaborate projections of the impact of different rates on water quality. Self-monitoring, regulated through random checks by government inspectors and criminal penalties for false reporting, provides information on discharge levels. Each source's charge is calculated on the basis of total yearly discharges, but paid in equal monthly installments. A penalty of 0.1 percent of the charge is levied for every day the payment is late.

Since at least the 1960s Allen Kneese and others have been advocating a program of effluent charges geared to the achievement of water quality goals.[17] While the program was not distilled into a specific legislative proposal, its elements have been discussed in a number of publications. The approach is discussed in chapter 2 and so only the briefest summary will be given here. Charges

---

[16] Irwin and Liroff, *Economic Disincentives*, p. 113.

[17] Allen V. Kneese and Blair T. Bower, *Managing Water Quality: Economics, Technology, and Institutions* (Baltimore, Johns Hopkins University Press for Resources for the Future, 1968).

would be set on one or a few pollution indicators, such as BOD. The rates would be set separately for each river basin to achieve the desired level of water quality for that basin. Initial charge rates would be calculated using marginal control cost data on classes of sources in the basin and appropriate hydrological models so as to come as close as possible to the "correct" charge. The charge scheme would be supplemented by regulatory controls where discharge prohibitions were more appropriate, as with toxic substances.

Two specific legislative proposals for water quality-oriented effluent charges were made in Maine in the early 1970s. One has been associated with A. Myrick Freeman,[18] the other with Orlando Delogu.[19] Both systems were designed to attain water quality standards and provide revenue for water pollution control administration and treatment subsidies.

Under the Delogu proposal, charges were to apply only to dischargers to stream segments in which water quality standards were violated. The charges were to be set by prorating the total capital and operating costs of meeting the standards in each such segment among all dischargers to the segment based on the quality and quantities of their discharges. Under the Freeman proposal, on the other hand, all sources except municipalities were to pay charges of 10¢ per pound of total noncarbonate carbons, 3¢ per pound of total suspended solids, and 25¢ per million Btu's of thermal energy. The rates could be increased by regulation up to statutorily prescribed maxima where they proved to be too low to result in achievement of the water quality goals.

The two programs were to have some significant administrative differences. The Freeman scheme relied on discharger monitoring while the Delogu proposal appears to have left that function to the state agency. To ensure prompt collection of charges, the Freeman proposal called for, among other things, the state to obtain liens on nonpayers' property, while the Delogu proposal required the state to subtract charge amounts overdue from municipalities from any state aid to such towns and cities.

18 Maine Legislature, Legislative Document No. 1450 (1971).
19 Orlando E. Delogu, "A Statutory Approach to Effluent Charges," *Maine Law Review* vol. 23, no. 2 (1971) p. 281.

Charges to Finance Collective Control Measures

A number of charge systems are designed to achieve water quality objectives for complete river basins by financing collective control measures designed to clean up the rivers to the desired levels. The most notable system of this type is run by private associations of dischargers in the Ruhr valley in West Germany. Municipal sewer user charges are the closest the United States has come to this approach to water pollution control, but there have been several proposals that adhere more closely to the Ruhr example.[20]

The Ruhr river basin associations build and operate regional treatment facilities, systems for flow augmentation, and facilities which reaerate the rivers themselves. Some rivers are used as sewers to carry wastes to central treatment facilities; others are kept clean in accord with regional plans. All these activities are paid for from charge revenues.

The costs are allocated among dischargers on the basis of a single unitary measure of treatment difficulty and cost. For example, one association uses the "population equivalent of biological oxygen demand," that is, the average BOD generated by one adult in one day, as the measure. The toxicity of substances in the effluent is also taken into account. The total costs of control are divided among dischargers proportionally on the basis of their shares of the total load of BOD population equivalents and toxics discharged.

The associations' monitoring costs are kept down by using somewhat crude measures that are easy to administer. Discharge levels are inferred from production figures on the basis of established

[20] The West German government and France have instituted charge systems that are apparently modeled on the Ruhr approach (Irwin and Liroff, *Economic Disincentives*). In addition, the Netherlands has instituted a somewhat different system of charges on chemical oxygen demand in effluents that is designed to generate revenues to finance pollution control measures by government and by individual sources. For discussion, see *Problems of the Human Environment in the Netherlands: A National Report*, United Nations Conference on the Human Environment, Stockholm, June 1972, F/4107/71, pp. 60–61 and Irwin and Liroff, *Economic Disincentives*, p. 115.

Senator Proxmire introduced a charges proposal (the Regional Water Quality Act of 1971) that was designed to provide revenue for regional and local water pollution control efforts, but the charges were to be uniform nationwide and not tied to water quality (*Congressional Record of Proceedings and Debate of the 92nd Congress, 1st Session* vol. 117, no. 164, for Tuesday, November 2, 1971, pp. 517425–32).

production functions. For example, it might be determined that a brewery using a given process would generate 5 population equivalents of wastes per barrel of beer produced. Where the discharger's process changes or improved treatment measures enable it to perform better than the production function would indicate, it has the burden of proving its lower discharges. Occasional discharge sampling is done by association staff to help maintain the accuracy of the system. Disputes over the discharge figures used in calculating the charge are resolved in an appeal process. That process reportedly works smoothly, in part because the agency levying the charges is made up of representatives of dischargers; it is not a government agency that might be perceived as an adversary. Note the parallel with the Japanese compensation law, covered in the section on air pollution, which has been an administrative success partly because of a high level of involvement by organizations representing those charged.

Municipal sewage treatment user charges, which are mandated in the United States by the Federal Water Pollution Control Act for towns receiving federal sewer system construction grants, are a domestic example of charges used to finance collective control activities. Those municipalities receiving the federal money are required to recover their operating costs from their users (industrial users are also required to pay a share of capital costs).

Several different charge formulas are used in the existing U.S. sewer user charge program. The differences are important, because they present users with very different incentives and municipalities with different monitoring responsibilities. *Ad valorem* taxes that increase users' property taxes in proportion to their prior tax rates are one example. With this approach the individual user's tax does not vary with the size of its waste contribution. As a result, there is no incentive to cut down on discharges to the municipal system, but there is also no need to incur the cost to monitor discharges from the many homes and factories connected to the system.

Another approach allocates costs on the basis of the volume of wastes from different sources as measured by water intake. Treatment costs vary with the volume, concentration, and nature of substances in the waste stream. This means that in a volume-based charge, costs may not be allocated in proportion to the user's con-

tribution to them. Furthermore, the incentive created by such a charge is to cut down water intake, which will not necessarily cut the quantity of wastes discharged. On the other hand, water intake is generally already metered so that monitoring is not a problem.

Two other approaches that avoid the incentive problems but add to the monitoring problems are unit price charges and sewer surcharges. Unit price charges are based on the volume of wastes delivered and on the amount of specific pollutants included. Sewer surcharges combine the volume approach and the unit charge approach. Charges are based on volume alone unless the concentrations of specific pollutants exceed base levels. Surcharges are levied on the excess concentrations. These two approaches resemble classic effluent charges in that they vary with the amount of certain pollutants discharged and create an incentive to control discharges.

Sewer user charges differ from the other systems in this category because they are not linked directly to achievement of water quality goals. A system closer to the Ruhr model in that regard was proposed for use in this country by Marc Roberts.[21] The Roberts proposal would have given centralized river basin authorities the responsibility of achieving water quality goals for each basin. The authorities would implement basin-wide pollution control programs and finance their activities with charges based on the marginal costs of adding the source to the basin-wide control system.

A charge system like that used in the Ruhr or proposed by Roberts has several interesting aspects. First, it reduces the short-term uncertainty about water quality levels that exists with charge schemes in the first category discussed above. An agency need not levy a charge and wait to see what effect it has on discharger control decisions and water quality. Instead, it plans direct action to control pollution to desired levels and then levies the charge to finance the controls.

Second, the approach permits antipollution measures or economies of scale not likely to be utilized under systems which rely on actions by individual polluters. Centralized treatment facilities, flow augmentation, and reaeration may be economically more efficient than controlling sources individually in many cases. Indi-

---

[21] Marc J. Roberts, "River Basin Authorities: A National Solution to Water Pollution," *Harvard Law Review* vol. 83 (1970) pp. 1527–56.

vidual sources would experience difficulty in organizing to take advantage of these opportunities. On the other hand, there is also a risk that regional agencies, eager to perpetuate their existence and increase their budgets, might emphasize large-scale measures, even when they offered no advantage over action by individual sources.

Third, despite the emphasis upon the collective approach, such charges do provide an incentive for individual sources to control their discharges (if the charge varies with the size of the discharge). The experience in the Ruhr and in the United States with user charges indicates that incentive-based decreases in discharges may be stimulated, although the scope of this effect has not been calculated. In the Ruhr, pretreatment by individual sources subject to the charges is common, but the extent to which the charges are responsible for the result is not clear, because conventional regulatory programs also have an effect. The imposition of user charges in a number of U.S. cities (preeminent examples include Springfield, Missouri and Otsego, Michigan) resulted in significant control efforts by industries discharging to the municipal sewer system. A review of broad studies of industrial responses to the imposition of user charges suggested that while industries are quite sensitive to the initial imposition of a charge, they may not respond nearly as much to changes in the charge level.[22]

Charges in Conjunction with Effluent Standards

Charges can be used as an effective adjunct to regulatory systems that feature effluent standards. Examples of this approach can be seen in charges programs in East Germany and Hungary and in two proposals for charges in the United States.[23] These systems can

22 Urban Systems Research & Engineering, Inc., "The Distribution of Water Pollution Control Costs: The Municipal Industrial Interface." Prepared for the National Commission on Water Quality, August 26, 1975, pp. 25–30.

23 A short-lived U.S. charges program is somewhat related to this category. In 1969 Vermont enacted an effluent charge law to back up its permit program. (Vermont Statutes Annotated, vol. 10, ch. 33, §§901–920.) The law required dischargers holding temporary permits (pending completion of abatement measures) to pay charges until the control measures were completed. The charges were to be based on the economic damage caused by discharges. It was never implemented, in large part because of the practical difficulty of measuring economic damage.

be viewed either as regulatory programs in which charges play an enforcement role, or as bona fide charges systems in which specified discharge levels have been exempted from the charge. However they are characterized, these mixed systems illustrate that effluent charges and effluent standards are not mutually exclusive pollution control instruments.

East Germany[24] and Hungary[25] have enacted water pollution control programs combining charges and effluent standards. Both countries levy charges on all discharges in excess of fixed effluent standards. The Hungarian charges are based on the costs of attaining the discharge standards, taking into account the condition of the receiving waters and other factors as well. The revenue from the East German charge is directed into abatement, environmental improvement measures, and compensation to some pollution victims. Unlike many charge schemes discussed in this chapter, which rely on self-monitoring by sources with random spot checks by the regulators, the Hungarian system appears to rely solely on discharge sampling by the government for its monitoring data. The Hungarian charges initially had little effect, but after they were raised, an upsurge in installation of treatment systems followed.

Two proposals have been developed in some detail that would amend the Federal Water Pollution Control Act and its effluent standards approach to include charges. Under both proposals, the 1977 (best practicable technology) effluent standards would remain in force, but the 1983 (best available technology) standards would be replaced with effluent charges. One program was proposed by Meta Systems,[26] a Cambridge, Massachusetts, consulting firm; the other was suggested by Blair Bower and Allen Kneese.[27]

The Meta Systems and Bower–Kneese systems have somewhat different purposes. The former is designed to achieve the same

24 Sand, "The Socialist Response," and Irwin and Liroff, *Economic Disincentives*, pp. 111–112.

25 Sand, "The Socialist Response," pp. 476–478.

26 "Effluent Charges: Is the Price Right?" Meta Systems, Inc., Cambridge, Mass. (September 1973).

27 Blair T. Bower, "Economic Incentives and Disincentives in REQM." Paper prepared for the National Academy of Sciences; Blair T. Bower and Allen V. Kneese, "Residuals–Environmental Quality Management: Economic, Technological, Ecological, and Institutional Aspects of Residuals Management." Report on a research program prepared for Resources for the Future, Washington, D.C., 1975.

level of ambient quality as would the 1983 standards, but using a charge mechanism. The latter system has a more limited purpose. It is intended to establish the principle of polluters paying for their use of public resources and to provide incentives to enhance abatement levels after achievement of the 1977 standards. The 1983 water quality levels would apparently not necessarily be achieved.

In the Meta Systems program, a separate, unitary charge rate would be set for each river basin. It would be calculated using information on the costs of abatement for different types of sources and the hydrology and other characteristics of the particular waterway in question. The charge paid by an individual source would be a product of the appropriate charge rate and the amount of pollutant it discharged, as measured by an index of pollutant strength called the "biomass potential." To minimize the financial impact of the charges, a portion of each discharge (calculated so as not to reduce the abatement incentive) would be exempted. Other special features would protect municipalities from heavy financial burdens, particularly small municipalities which tend to have relatively high per capita treatment costs.

The Bower–Kneese system is quite different. It calls for a uniform nationwide charge (or charges, if more than one substance or measure is covered). States would be free to add charges to the national base, however, to provide local flexibility. Charges would be levied only on discharges over the amount allowed by the 1977 standards. Like the Meta Systems approach, abatement cost information would provide the basis for the level of the charges rate, and a discharge index would be used to measure an individual source's charge liability. The charges would vary with seasonal changes in the assimilative capacity of the receiving waters. The Bower–Kneese system also calls for a special charge rate (double or triple the normal one) for discharges exceeding a daily maximum (to combat pulse discharges).

According to their proponents, the Meta Systems and Bower–Kneese approaches would have several beneficial effects on the federal water pollution control program. They would scrap the heavily contested 1983 standards. The charges would be a useful new program tool that would: (1) make the program more efficient from an economic perspective; (2) make the program more

effective because sources would have an immediate economic incentive to take pollution control steps; (3) make the program more suitable to the dynamic reality of pollution control because it is more easily adjusted to changes in abatement techniques and economics, and (4) make the program more useful for future policy decision making because it would generate hard data on abatement costs.

Solid Wastes

Solid waste disposal is a major environmental problem that has important economic roots. The forces that produce waste can in large measure be traced to an economic system that fosters high rates of consumption. Raw material depletion allowances contribute to use of virgin materials rather than recycled ones. Products are built to have short life spans, while large quantities of packaging are used to help sell products. Manufacturers and merchandisers reap a large share of the benefits of these and similar policies, but have to bear only a small share of the environmental costs. A number of charge systems have been developed that seek to redress this problem of externalities.[28]

Beverage Container Deposits

Beverage container deposit systems are a form of solid waste charge that has attracted attention nationwide. The deposits, paid by consumers, are refunded when empty bottles or cans are returned to retail outlets. Thus, the person who buys a soft drink or beer and adds the container to the solid waste stream in effect pays a charge, and the person who picks up and returns the discarded container is paid a bounty.

Oregon,[29] Vermont,[30] Michigan,[31] and Maine[32] have instituted beverage container deposit programs.[33] The Oregon program,

[28] For a recent discussion of solid waste disposal charges, see OECD, *Pollution Charges*.

[29] Charles M. Gudger and Kenneth M. Walters, "Beverage Container Regulation: Economic Implications and Suggestions for Model Legislation," *Ecology Law Quar-*

which has been the model for most proposals, and the established Vermont scheme are the focus of this discussion.

These two states have taken somewhat different approaches but both combine economic incentives and regulatory prohibitions for certain types of containers. Oregon requires deposits of 2¢ on containers that are reusable by more than one manufacturer, and deposits of 5¢ on all other containers. The deposits are refunded when the empty containers are returned. Cans with detachable tab openers are banned. Vermont, on the other hand, requires refundable deposits of 5¢ on all beer and soft drink containers. Throwaway bottles, cans with detachable tab openers, and can and bottle carriers that are not biodegradable are prohibited.

The administration of beverage container refund systems could be complex, since the deposits and refunds are handled by retailers. Vermont requires bottle and can manufacturers to pay 1¢ per container to retailers to finance their increased handling responsibilities.

Perhaps as a result of the intense opposition mounted by bottle and can manufacturers and economically related groups, the actual and potential impacts of beverage container charge systems have been subjected to widespread, detailed study. The studies indicate that the systems can be quite effective in reducing the bottle and can component of solid wastes, with limited adverse overall economic effects. In Oregon the system has resulted in a marked shift to refillable bottles. For instance, refillable beer bottles increased

---

terly vol. 5, no. 2 (1976) p. 265. Also, *Oregon Laws of 1971*, ch. 745, O.R.S. §§459, 810 et seq.

30 Irwin and Liroff, *Economic Disincentives*, pp. 88–92.

31 "Michigan and Maine Pass Bottle Laws," *Environmental Law Review* vol. 6 (1976) p. 10273.

32 Ibid.

33 Several localities have done so as well, but these programs have generally not been implemented due to legal challenges. ["Questions and Answers: Returnable Beverage Containers for Beer and Soft Drinks" (Washington, EPA, July 1975).]

There have also been proposals for instituting deposit/refund programs in other states and localities, on a nationwide basis and for federal facilities. [Statement of the Hon. John R. Quarles, Jr., Deputy Administrator, Environmental Protection Agency, Before the Subcommittee on the Environment of the Senate Committee on Commerce (1974); EPA, "Proposed Solid Waste Management Guidelines, Beverage Containers," *Federal Register* vol. 40 (1975) p. 52968; "Beverage Container Guidelines for Federal Agencies, Commentary," last revision (Washington, EPA, January 26, 1976).]

from 31 percent to 96 percent of the market. Bottle and can litter decreased by over 65 percent in both Oregon and Vermont in the year after the deposit and refund schemes went into effect.[34]

Because refillable bottles require less energy to produce and use than one-way bottles and cans, the shift away from throwaways is expected to result in substantial savings of energy. A Connecticut study estimated that a deposit scheme there could result in savings of from 13 to 20 million gallons of fuel oil equivalent annually.[35] On a national basis the projected savings are also large (218 trillion Btu's in one EPA study).[36]

The Connecticut study indicated that beer and soft drink prices would go down slightly, that sales volume would remain the same, and that an overall increase in employment and income in the state would result. Increased employment in retail establishments and beverage handling firms was expected to more than offset declines in can and bottle manufacturing jobs. A study of the projected impact of a nationwide deposit scheme anticipated an overall increase in jobs, accompanied by a decrease in income which would result from a shift from manufacturing to lower-paying retail jobs.[37]

Beverage container deposit systems can be contrasted with another charges-type proposal aimed at bottles and cans. A tax on bottles and cans (not associated with a ban on any nonreturnables) used to finance litter cleanup has been instituted in the state of Washington.[38] The tax rate, 0.15 mills per container, is much lower than the deposits required in Oregon and Vermont. The tax creates no incentive against littering since it is paid regardless of what eventually happens to the can or bottle. Furthermore, the tax rate is the same for returnable and nonreturnable containers and would not encourage use of refillable bottles. Such a tax pays for

[34] EPA, "Questions and Answers."

[35] Carlos Stern, Testimony Before the Environment Committee, Connecticut State Legislature, February 24, 1976.

[36] Resource Recovery and Waste Reduction. Third Report to Congress (Washington, EPA, 1975) p. 23.

[37] Statement of the Hon. John R. Quarles, Jr., Deputy Administrator, Environmental Protection Agency, Before the Subcommittee on the Environment of the Senate Committee on Commerce (1974) p. 9.

[38] Washington Laws of 1971, ch. 307, S.B. 428-X. Telephone interview with Bob Evers, Can Manufacturers Institute, December 9, 1976.

cleanup of litter after it occurs but does nothing to reduce the amount of litter or the volume of bottles and cans that enter the solid waste stream.

Product Charges

The financial and environmental costs of solid waste collection and disposal by towns have begun to reach crisis levels and the charges concept has been adapted to this problem generally.

New York City[39] attempted to combat some aspects of the solid waste problem with a recycling incentive tax, which was designed for a variety of packaging materials and enacted for plastics. The tax scheme was never fully implemented due to a legal challenge, but it provides a detailed example of a possible approach. Both the U.S. Senate Subcommittee on Environmental Pollution[40] and EPA[41] have given similar systems detailed consideration. The Senate Subcommittee held hearings on legislation on "product disposal charges" drafted by Senator Gary Hart in May 1976, while EPA's 1976 *Fourth Report to Congress* contains a lengthy discussion of "product charges."

The New York City recycling incentive tax and the national product disposal charge schemes have similar goals. They are intended to reduce cities' solid waste loads by encouraging shifts to packaging materials (a major constituent of solid wastes) that can be recycled or reused. Furthermore, both approaches are designed to provide money to municipalities to help offset disposal costs.

The recycling incentive tax and the product disposal charges are structured differently, in part because the jurisdictions of the implementing governments are vastly different in scope. The New York City tax was to be levied on New York City retailers and

39 "A Recycling Incentive Tax," McKinsey & Co., Report for New York City Bureau of the Budget (November 1971).

40 *Hearings to Consider the Effects of Product Disposal Charges on Municipal Waste Recovery and Reuse Before the Panel on Metals Policy of the Subcommittee on Environmental Pollution of the Senate Committee on Public Works*, 94 Cong., 2 sess. (1976).

41 *An Evaluation of Product Charges as a National Solid Waste Management Tool.* Fourth Report to Congress (Washington, EPA) ch. 8 (Draft, June 22, 1976); Richard Slitor, "Administrative Aspects of a Dedicated Manufacturers Excise Tax on Solid Waste-Creating Products." A report for the Resources Recovery Division, Environmental Protection Agency (June 15, 1976).

wholesalers of packaged products. This would entail significant administrative costs. On the other hand, the product disposal charge schemes would tax bulk producers or importers of packaging materials. One study indicated that the number of tax returns for a national system such as this would be only 9,240 or about 0.7 percent of the number of federal excise tax returns processed annually by the Internal Revenue Service. A single municipality, of course, could not employ such an approach, because its jurisdiction would extend at most to manufacturers and bulk distributors of only a small proportion of the packaging eventually discarded by its residents.

The recycling incentive tax rates were designed to create price differentials favoring containers that do not create serious solid waste problems. The rates vary by category of container, depending on the extent to which recycled materials have been used in producing the packaging and the ease with which futher recycling or reuse could be accomplished. For instance, under the original proposal, plastic bottles which are nondegradable and compression resistant were to be charged at the highest rate per container (3¢). Multimetallic containers (2¢) were to be charged at a higher rate than monometallic containers (1¢), reflecting differences in recycling ease. Credits of 1¢ per container were to be allowed for reusable containers or containers made with prescribed amounts of recycled materials.

The product disposal charges would be based directly on disposal costs. Base charges would be $26 per ton for various kinds of packaging material (based on the national average direct cost of municipal solid waste collection, disposal, etc.). A $3 per ton surcharge has been considered, because $3 per ton of solid wastes is the estimated average additional cost of upgrading an environmentally unsound landfill to meet present standards. The charge rate would be revised every two to four years.

Senator Gary Hart's proposal has several provisions that create recycling and other waste-saving incentives. The charge program would allow exemptions for the weight of recycled materials used in the charged packaging. It would also establish a subsidy (in addition to the charge exemption) for use of recycled materials in packaging. The subsidy would be phased out over ten years. It is intended to provide a strong initial boost to the development of

markets in recycled materials and to soften adverse effects of the charge on employment.

The revenue from the New York and national schemes would be used somewhat differently, but would benefit municipalities in all cases. In the New York program the money went into general revenues. In Senator Hart's product disposal charge system, a small part of the revenue would go to cover administrative costs, then recycling subsidies would be paid and all remaining money would go to municipalities. The EPA product charge study suggests that revenues go to municipalities via direct revenue sharing.

Other Solid Waste Charges

Several other charges solutions to solid waste problems have been suggested in at least general terms. One proposal is to tax products in proportion to their useful life or virgin material content.[42] Another proposal is to reduce or eliminate the depletion allowances that favor extraction of virgin materials. (Some states already have severance taxes on certain virgin materials, thus reducing the impact of depletion allowances.[43]) All these schemes would create financial incentives to recycle materials and to build more durable products and might help combat the throwaway ethic that permeates our economic system.

Land Use

A number of states and at least one foreign country are using their tax policies to fight the irrational development of rural land. Once again the problem can be viewed as one of externalities. The transformation of farmland into shopping centers or scenic wilderness areas into ski resorts creates costs for society that are not borne by those involved in the changeover. The sale or lease of rural land for development provides a convenient access point for government to include at least some elements of overall social cost in

[42] Norman Dean, *Energy Efficiency in Industry: A Guide to Legal Barriers and Opportunities* (New York, Ballinger, forthcoming).

[43] National Conference of State Legislatures, Energy Report to the States: State Energy Taxation (1976).

Tax Percentage on Land Sales

| Number of years | Percentage of Gain Realized | | |
held by transferor	0–99	100–199	200 or more
Less than 1	30	45	60
1 to 2	25	37.5	50
2 to 3	20	30	40
3 to 4	15	22.5	30
4 to 5	10	15	20
5 to 6	5	7.5	10

the private land use calculus. The following paragraphs briefly describe four approaches to this problem.

Vermont taxes gains on land sales to discourage speculation in rural land.[44] The amount of the tax depends on the amount of gain realized and the length of time the land is held by the seller. As the following table indicates, the tax rate is quite high on quick, high-profit sales of land.

The law provides exemptions for land developed for residential homesites for the first purchaser or the next succeeding purchaser and excludes the portion of the sale price attributable to buildings on the land.

The administrative features of the Vermont land gains tax warrant special consideration. They illustrate how a charge or tax can be structured to minimize monitoring, collection, and enforcement costs. The law requires every land buyer to turn over 10 percent of the sale price to the state. The seller must file a return giving the data relevant to the tax amount. The state then issues a refund or collects any additional tax. The requirement for registering real estate transactions provides information on when a parcel of land has been sold and could provide leverage to ensure collection of the 10 percent tax prepayment. The prepayment gives the taxed party—the land seller—an incentive to supply the information necessary to calculate the tax, and eases collection problems.

[44] Vermont Land Gains Tax: Act 81 of the 1973 Vermont Laws, amending 32 V.S.A. §§5961, 5962(e), 5967–68, 5973; *adding* 32 V.S.A. §§5976–77 and 32 V.S.A. ch. 236, repealing 32 V.S.A. §5966. For a discussion of this tax see R. L. Baker, "Controlling Land Uses and Prices by Using Special Taxation to Intervene in the Land Market: The Vermont Experiment," *Environmental Affairs* vol. 4 (Summer 1975) pp. 427–480.

New York and Hawaii have adopted (and other states are considering) a simple approach to controlling development of farmland near urban areas.[45] Such land is assessed at preferentially low rates for property tax purposes while it is used for farming. This dampens the incentive of the farmer to sell and the developer to buy the land.

East Germany established a land use charge in 1967.[46] The charge applies to land removed permanently or temporarily from use for agriculture or forestry. It steers development to land that is relatively unsuited to such uses or ensures that temporary non-agrarian uses will not preclude return of the land to its former use. The charge amount is based on the productivity of the land. Revenue from the charge is used for land improvement measures and, if the land was used for mining, reclamation and recultivation.

Congestion

Charge systems have been implemented or proposed as means of remedying numerous kinds of congestion and crowding problems, many of which have environmental significance. Motor vehicle congestion in urban areas, crowding of parks, and costly demands on public transportation and airport landing facilities are all examples of problems to which the charges approach has proven to be applicable in theory or practice.

Urban Motor Vehicle Congestion Charges

Consider motor vehicle congestion.[47] During peak use periods traffic slows to a crawl. Cars and trucks contribute a large share of the air and noise pollution of the cities, and do their worst damage during the traffic jams of misnamed "rush hour" periods. Car pools and buses are vastly outnumbered by automobiles carrying only one person each, a fact that contributes to congestion and

---

45 Letter from Charles N. Ehler to Frederick R. Anderson, May 18, 1976.

46 Sand, "The Socialist Response," pp. 475–476.

47 For a discussion of the problem of vehicular congestion and its relation to energy conservation, see Durwood J. Zaelke and Elizabeth Yu, *Saving Energy in Urban Transportation* (New York, Ballinger, forthcoming).

wastes energy. Finally, highways and parking lots necessary to handle the heavy traffic take up large amounts of valuable urban land. In the context of economic theory, driving in central cities at peak periods generates external costs because the total social costs created by traffic congestion greatly exceed the costs borne by riders in all the vehicles. The charges scheme most closely geared to the problem of vehicular congestion is a charge on driving in crowded center city areas during peak traffic hours. Such a charge has been implemented with apparent success in Singapore[48] and, it, in combination with three proposals for similar action elsewhere, provides a rich and thorough picture of the possible configurations of congestion charges. The three proposals include one for Los Angeles,[49] one for London,[50] and one by the Urban Institute[51] for a model city.

The Singapore, Urban Institute, Los Angeles, and London systems all have the primary purposes of reducing center city vehicular congestion and raising revenue. The Los Angeles proposal has the additional express purpose of reducing smog. Because of the well-established connection between congestion and other environmental problems, all four systems could be said to have the secondary purposes of reducing air pollution and noise, conserving energy, and limiting the need for new highway construction.

The four systems use somewhat different bases for their charge amounts. The Singapore charge is unique in that it is based on crude estimates of the monetary value to motorists of driving in the center city during peak hours. The Urban Institute and London charges are based solely on the costs of congestion in terms of estimates of the value of time lost. The Los Angeles proposal is also based on the costs of delay, but suggests that in addition, smog costs and hidden public service costs be taken into account as well.

[48] Peter L. Watson and Edward P. Holland, "Congestion Pricing—The Example of Singapore," in *Urban Transportation Pricing Alternatives*. Papers presented at a conference May 14–17, 1976, Easton, Md. (Transportation Research Board, National Academy of Sciences).

[49] Ward Elliott, "Road Use Charges and Jitneys: Some Thoughts on How to Introduce Them to L.A.," July 1976. (Claremont Men's College, Claremont, Calif.)

[50] A. D. May, "The London Supply Licensing Study," in *Urban Transportation Pricing Alternatives*. Papers presented at a conference May 14–17, 1976, Easton, Md. (Transportation Research Board, National Academy of Sciences, Review Draft).

[51] Kiran V. Bhatt, "What Can We Do About Urban Traffic Congestion? A Pricing Approach," The Urban Institute, Working Paper: 5032-03-1 (January 1975).

The variations in the charge formula in the four systems illustrate important tradeoffs between the sensitivity and effectiveness of the incentive created and the cost of effectively implementing the system. Some important variables include the specific activity charged, the types of vehicles charged, the area and location of the charge zone, the timing of the charge period, and the level and variability of the charge.

The system implemented in Singapore creates relatively few administrative problems at the cost of some limitation of its impact. Singapore's charge zone is a relatively small area that includes the most seriously congested downtown blocks, but excludes certain major thoroughfares needed as bypass routes for through traffic around the charge zone. The activity charged is limited to entering the zone during the morning rush hour. There are only twenty-two entry points, so traffic can be easily monitored. The charge is $1.30 per vehicle. All vehicles are charged except pool cars, emergency vehicles, and small commercial trucks (the lifeline of downtown businesses). The exemptions make the system somewhat more difficult to administer (e.g., pool cars must be distinguished from other cars at entry points) but avoid the creation of economic barriers to modes of transportation that contribute relatively little per passenger to congestion and vehicles that serve vital functions in the life of the city.

The proposed vehicle congestion charge systems for London and Los Angeles have more complex schemes than Singapore's. Los Angeles and London are less densely settled than Singapore, and thus their charge zones would have to be larger and have more entry and exit points to monitor. One London option provided for a 10-hour charge period and charges on driving within the charge zone as well as on entry and exit. This arrangement would obviously entail much greater administrative costs (e.g., monitoring for longer periods, at entry and exit points and all over the charge zone as well), but might be necessary to make the system work. London suffers serious congestion at lunch time as well as the morning and evening periods and a significant share of the traffic is made up of cars that are on trips entirely within the proposed charge zone or that originate in the zone and have destinations outside it. A Singapore-type charge would not discourage such trips at all.

Another possible variation is illustrated by the Los Angeles proposal. It would charge vehicles which enter the congested area during specified morning hours or which leave it during specified evening hours. The morning charge is different from the afternoon charge and both charges are different in the summer and winter, because the smog caused by congestion differs with the time of day and the season. The suggested charges are $1.25 upon entering the zone on a summer morning, 50¢ for leaving it on a summer evening or entering it on a winter morning, and 35¢ for leaving it on a winter evening. The price of such flexibility is more difficult and costly monitoring.

The Singapore program and all of the proposed schemes use a supplementary licensing system to help monitor chargeable driving and to collect the charges. The supplementary licensing system requires those wishing to drive in the charge zones to purchase and display windshield stickers. Thus the charge is collected before the charged conduct takes place. Only limited capital investment is needed for signs and perhaps for sticker sales booths. The Los Angeles proposal relegates this approach to a backup role in the long term, however, in favor of an automatic vehicle identification (AVI) system. The AVI system involves radio receivers at freeway ramps and other key points in the charge zone which sense the coming and going of vehicles through coded signals from radio transmitters in each car. Motorists are periodically billed for their trips in the charge zone. The AVI system makes it possible to monitor more vehicles with less delay and to more easily implement a variable charge. On the other hand, it entails substantial capital costs and raises troublesome questions about invasion of privacy.

A vehicle congestion charge alone is not necessarily enough to solve city traffic congestion. Singapore is a good example of a comprehensive approach. It established stiff parking surtaxes in the charge zone to further discourage automobile commuting and set up fringe parking lots and shuttle bus routes to make alternative transportation more attractive. The proposed systems also encourage alternatives. Notably, the Los Angeles scheme includes provisions for upgrading regular bus service and removing legal barriers to jitneys.

The potential effectiveness of congestion charges is demonstrated by the early results of the Singapore system. It cut morning peak traffic dramatically. The target was a 25–30 percent reduction in vehicles entering the charge zone during the charge period. The result of the charge, set without elaborate analysis of driver demand functions, was a 40 percent decline in total motor vehicles entering the charge zone during the charge period. The number of commercial vehicles (the smaller of which are not charged) actually increased slightly, while the number of autos entering the zone declined by 74 percent, enough to cut total traffic by 40 percent.

The charge had a number of side effects, some of which required additional action. Traffic in the half hour before the charge period increased by 23 percent. Because the volume of traffic in this peak was substantially below the precharge peak volume, and because it moved well, no corrective measures were taken. Initially, traffic also increased substantially in the period after the end of the charge period. Serious congestion resulted and the charge period was extended, eliminating the problem. Finally, there was very little decline in evening rush hour traffic in the charge zone. This is one of the costs of the simple, easy-to-administer charge design. Singapore officials apparently are planning a modification of the system, perhaps instituting an evening charge, to cut traffic in that period.

The charge provoked a shift to some other modes of transportation. Car pools increased by 82 percent. Bus ridership increased by 10–15 percent. However, very few motorists used the fringe parking/shuttle bus service set up in conjunction with the charge.

Finally, the Singapore system generated revenue at a $2 million per year rate in its early months. The proposed schemes should generate even more revenue. Projected revenue from the Urban Institute system (in a model city) is $54 million per year; from the Los Angeles, $400 million per year; and from the London proposal, $65 million to $146 million per year (depending on the charge configuration).

A variety of other charge systems that have been proposed to address the problems of vehicular congestion in cities deserve mention. Additional taxes on gasoline would increase the cost of driv-

ing and encourage the use of alternative transportation. Gas taxes, however, indiscriminately discourage driving. They do not focus on congestion. They are better viewed as general energy conservation measures than as anticongestion measures. Surcharges on downtown parking were briefly espoused at the national level by EPA and implemented in Singapore and San Francisco to discourage the use of cars in congestion-plagued urban areas.[52] Bridge and highway tolls are another means of combating congestion. Congestion tolls proposed for the Golden Gate Bridge[53] and urban expressways[54] are an example. Unfortunately, this approach cannot easily be applied to city streets. Toll booths themselves cause traffic tie-ups, unless they are very numerous. Large toll stations, in turn, require a great deal of land and capital, both of which are scarce in central cities.

Other Congestion Charges

The idea of congestion charges has been suggested for or applied to a variety of environmental problems in addition to those of motor traffic. These include overuse of parks, overconcentration of industry in urban areas, heavy plane traffic at airports, heavy boat traffic in inland waterways, and crowding on public transportation. These approaches all have one important characteristic in common with congestion charges for motor vehicles. All involve a system, facility, or environment that has costs generated by individual use during peak periods greater than the price charged for that use. In each area, pricing systems have been proposed or implemented that strike a better balance between the internal and external costs of peak period use.

[52] EPA started to set up a central business district parking surcharge, but retreated in the face of massive political opposition. (Irwin and Liroff, *Economic Disincentives*, pp. 139–145.) San Francisco instituted a downtown parking surcharge of 25 percent in 1970, but lowered the tax to 10 percent in 1972 due to political pressure. [Damian Kulash, "Parking Taxes as Roadway Prices: A Case Study of the San Francisco Experience." An Urban Institute paper (March 1974).]

[53] Ward Elliott, "The Case for Congestion Charges on the Golden Gate Bridge," paper (undated).

[54] Donald N. Dewees, "Travel, Cost, Transit and Control of Urban Motoring," *Public Policy* vol. 24, no. 1 (Winter 1976) p. 59.

Congestion pricing for the use of parks has been suggested in both the United States and Japan. A system of surcharges for use of park areas designated as crowded has been proposed in Japan.[55] The revenues would be used to finance measures to protect park areas against the effects of heavy use and to buy land for new or expanded parks. Congestion charges for parks and recreational facilities not heavily used by the poor have been proposed for the United States.[56] The present practice in California of charging a reduced fee for use of state parks in the offpeak fall, winter, and spring months is another example of congestion pricing for peak park use.

Congestion charges have also been applied in other areas. The Japanese have instituted a tax on industrial congestion.[57] Industries located in areas designated as overindustrialized pay a surtax designed to encourage them to relocate to less crowded areas. The revenues are used to help finance relocation and to provide incentives for rural areas to accept new industry.

Congestion charges have been implemented at a number of airports around the world. These charges are levied on landings during airport rush hours. They are designed to even the flow of traffic, in part by providing an incentive for private aircraft to use the airports during relative lulls in commercial traffic. Such charges have been instituted at airports in the New York metropolitan area.[58] Landing charges for private aircraft were raised to the level paid by commercial aircraft during peak periods. The result was a significant shift in the airport usage patterns of such aircraft and a decrease in congestion. Landing charges have also been instituted at Heathrow Airport in London, with equally beneficial results in cutting congestion.[59] Airport congestion charges must be distin-

[55] Koichiro Fujikura, "A Memorandum on Environmentally Oriented Charges in Japan," May 8, 1976, pp. 3–4.

[56] John V. Krutilla and Jack L. Knetsch, "Outdoor Recreation Economics," *The Annals of the American Academy of Political and Social Sciences* vol. 389 (May 1970) pp. 63–70.

[57] Fujikura, "Memorandum," pp. 4–5.

[58] Ward Elliott, "Road Use Charges," p. 11. Letter from Ward Elliott to Frederick R. Anderson, June 17, 1976. Letter from Albert J. Rosenthal to Frederick R. Anderson, June 1, 1976.

[59] Ward Elliott, "Road Use Charges." Letter from Albert J. Rosenthal to Frederick R. Anderson, June 1, 1976.

guished from airport noise charges, which have also been implemented in a number of cities and are discussed below.

Peak load pricing on the use of public transportation is another
application of the approach used in highway congestion pricing.
Rush hour surcharges on the Washington, D.C. Metro (and in
D.C. taxis) and Amtrak offpeak discounts for rail travel are examples of this approach. They are designed to provide an incentive
for passengers to shift from peak periods when capacity is overused, to other periods when capacity is currently underused.[60]

Noise

High noise levels in cities and factories, near construction sites and
highways, and elsewhere are serious environmental problems. As
with many other environmental problems, the costs of noise are
often externalities. The manufacturers and users of motor vehicles,
jet airplanes, and factory equipment bear only a small share of the
costs which their noise imposes on society. The charges concept
has received attention as a means of redressing this economic
imbalance.

A number of noise control charge systems have been developed
or implemented around the world.[61] Charges on airplane noise
have been enacted (though not implemented) in Japan,[62] proposed
for the Netherlands,[63] and endorsed by the Organisation for Economic Co-operation and Development (OECD).[64] Noise from highway traffic is the subject of proposed charges in the Netherlands[65]

[60] A similar situation exists in other industries such as electric utilities and phone
companies which must have a great deal of service capacity in order to handle peak
loads, but which are underused much of the time. Special reduced rates for offpeak
long-distance calls and long-term marginal cost pricing of electricity share the
rationale of congestion charges.

[61] For a recent discussion of solid waste disposal charges, see OECD, *Pollution
Charges.*

[62] Fujikura, "Memorandum," pp. 1–3.

[63] "Noise Charges in the Netherlands," Ad Hoc Group on Noise Abatement Policies (Panel 2), OECD, Environmental Directorate, Paris, April 2, 1976. English text.
Working paper 2.

[64] *The Washington Post*, June 27, 1976, p. F1; "Charging for Noise," Ad Hoc
Group on Noise Abatement Policies (Panel 2), OECD, Environmental Directorate,
Paris, February 23, 1976, English text. Working paper 1.

[65] OECD, "Noise Charges in the Netherlands."

and is a secondary target of the highway congestion charges discussed elsewhere in this chapter. Finally, the Netherlands is also considering legislation setting charges on other sources of noise, factories, construction equipment, and the like.[66]

Airport Noise Charges

This subsection compares the airport noise charges system of Japan and those proposed for the Netherlands and by the OECD.[67] There is a basic difference between the Japanese and Dutch systems on the one hand and the OECD approach on the other. The Japanese and Dutch charge schemes are designed to reduce the impact of airport noise on surrounding residential neighborhoods by financing soundproofing, or the relocation of families. The OECD proposal, however, is designed to create an incentive for airlines to use quieter aircraft and develop new noise control technologies, and to provide revenue to compensate victims of airport noise. We see again the alternatives of charges to finance government action to correct an environmental problem and charges to create an incentive for those causing the problem to control their activities.

The basis of the Japanese and Dutch charges is the cost of measures to reduce the impact of airport noise. In the Dutch proposal, the charge base includes the costs of soundproofing dwellings to achieve areawide noise standards where possible, of the demolition of houses and the relocation of families where the standards cannot be met, and of administering the charge system. Charges are levied on each aircraft landing. They are set so as to recoup the total cost of noise impact reduction measures and vary according to the decibel level typically generated by the type of plane used. The Dutch proposal adds another wrinkle: it charges a higher rate for night landings on the theory that they cause greater annoyance.

The proposed OECD approach is different and somewhat more complicated. It combines performance standards and charges in a way designed to produce several interesting incentive effects. A

---

[66] Ibid.

[67] A study commission has recommended that airport noise charges be adapted for use in Boston's Logan Airport. Letter from Albert J. Rosenthal to Frederick R. Anderson, June 1, 1976.

noise standard, in decibels, is set for each type of jet aircraft. The standard is at a level lower than could be attained by adding the best available noise control equipment to the jet engines of that type of plane in order to create a continuing incentive to improve aircraft noise control technology.

Each type of jet plane is also rated as to its noise level with lesser or no controls. Every time a jet aircraft lands, its owners must pay a charge. The charge is equal to a per decibel rate, multiplied by the number of decibels by which the noise rating of that type of plane (with whatever noise controls have been installed) exceeds the standard. Since all planes' noise ratings exceed the appropriate standards, some charge will have to be paid on every landing. This charge creates the incentive for noise control innovation.

The per decibel charge rate is set high enough to induce the use of the best "retrofit" noise control on all aircraft for which it is available. It is based on the total costs of such control (including capital, installation, maintenance, reduced payloads, and so on) for the type of aircraft for which those costs are highest. All types of planes are charged at the same rate so it should always be cheaper to install noise controls than to pay the charge.

It is interesting that the projected level of the Netherlands charge would not be high enough to induce the use of existing noise control technology by airlines.[68] Thus the charge would benefit only people living near airports, and those persons only while they are in their homes. By contrast, the OECD charges would benefit a wider class of people, because they would reduce the noise generated by aircraft, but would also cost airlines and travelers more money than the other schemes.

There are differences in the use of revenues between the Japanese/Dutch systems and the OECD approach. The former uses the money to finance government measures to lessen the impact of aircraft noise. The latter dedicates the revenue to the compensation of noise victims, not to government action to protect them from noise. Presumably, the noise victims would have the choice of using the money for soundproofing, relocation, or other goods and services which they value more highly than reduced noise levels. All three systems would use the revenue to pay the cost of adminis-

[68] OECD, "Noise Charges in the Netherlands," p. 45.

tering the charges program. The charges should generate substantial revenue. The OECD estimated that its system could raise up to $42 million per year if used at London's Heathrow Airport.

Much of the administrative cost of the aircraft noise control charges seems to stem from the way the revenue is used. The administration of these systems provokes several comments. Collection should be a minor problem, because the noise charges are simply added to landing fees already collected by airport authorities. However, the government antinoise measures (e.g., relocation of families) of the Japanese and Netherlands systems and, to a lesser extent, the noise victim compensation system of the OECD proposal (e.g., screening claimants for compensation) may entail a heavy administrative burden.

Road Traffic Noise Control

Two charges-oriented systems have been suggested in the Netherlands for controlling highway traffic noise.[69] Both charges would be collected on the sale or registration of motor vehicles. They differ in the same way the airport noise charge of the OECD differs from those of Japan and the Netherlands. One charge is designed to finance governmental actions to cut noise impact near highways, the other to create an incentive for car manufacturers to produce (and for drivers to purchase) quieter cars.

In the system designed to finance noise control, the charge would be based on the cost of such measures as leaving noise buffer zones between highways and homes, and soundproofing buildings. Only persons who lived near highways would benefit, unless the charges happened to be high enough to prod auto makers into producing quieter cars. Charge levels would be set by allocating the total cost of the noise control measures on the basis of noise levels of different types of vehicles under test conditions. Problems with this approach are the difficulty of setting precise standards for such a variable phenomenon as noise and the complexity of determining the costs of achieving those standards.

In the system designed to produce an abatement incentive, the charge would be based on the cost of vehicle noise abatement

[69] OECD, "Charging for Noise," "Noise Charges in the Netherlands."

technology and perhaps the cost of research and development to improve that technology. These charges would vary from one vehicle type to another, depending on their tested noise levels. A stumbling block for this approach is the lack of information about motor vehicle noise abatement costs. Furthermore, the Netherlands comprises only a small portion of the market for most manufacturers of motor vehicles. Thus the incentive may not be sufficient to create the desired effect on most car and truck manufacturers.

Other Noise Charges

The Netherlands is also the source of proposed legislation setting up other charges aimed at factories and "apparatuses" that are noisy.[70] One charge levied on both factories and "apparatuses" is intended to generate revenue for administration of a broad, largely regulatory, noise control program. The other charge would be applied to "apparatuses" that fail to meet noise standards.

Energy

The charges approach figures prominently in programs being developed to respond to the increasingly apparent limited availability of energy-producing resources.[71] The main thrust of the proposals that have been made is simply to raise the price of energy, thus reducing the rate of consumption. The proposals can be divided into direct and indirect energy charges.

Direct Energy Charges

A number of proposals have been raised that would conserve energy by directly making it more expensive. Taxes or surtaxes on gasoline,[72] natural gas,[73] and electricity[74] or other nonrenewable

[70] OECD, "Noise Charges in the Netherlands."

[71] The problems of energy conservation are dealt with in much greater depth than is possible here in a series of books by the Energy Conservation Project of the Environmental Law Institute soon to be published by Ballinger Press.

[72] Ward Elliott, "VMT Disincentive Choices for the L.A. Basin," paper (undated);

resources[75] have been suggested. To have a reasonably predictable effect on energy consumption, such taxes would have to be based on energy demand functions. Care would have to be exercised in designing the tax systems to ensure that they did not simply shift consumption to other sources of energy that are equally scarce or that give rise to major secondary costs in terms of pollution and highly destructive extraction processes.

Another energy-saving measure that has some similarity to charges fits into this category. It is long-term marginal cost pricing of energy. This approach would match the price of energy (e.g., electricity) more closely with the actual costs of producing it. This would be an improvement over the widespread present pricing approach that gives discounts to heavy peak period users, even though peak period service is more expensive to provide and can result in excessive capital investment. Like other charge systems discussed in this chapter, long-term marginal cost pricing is designed to correct a pricing system that encourages unnecessarily heavy use of scarce resources.

Indirect Energy Charges

Charges in this category function somewhat differently from direct energy charges. Rather than raising the price of energy, the proposed charges raise the price of products whose production or use consumes large quantities of energy. Included in this category are a tax on consumer products based on the energy input required for their manufacture,[76] a tax or higher utility rate for buildings that fail to meet insulation standards,[77] and taxes on motor vehicles that are based on horsepower,[78] fuel efficiency,[79] or mileage driven.[80]

Donald N. Dewees, "Travel, Cost, Transit and Control of Urban Motoring," *Public Policy* vol. 24, no. 1 (Winter 1976) pp. 74–75.

[73] Dean, *Energy Efficiency*.

[74] Ibid.

[75] Letter from Laurence I. Moss to Frederick R. Anderson, undated.

[76] Dean, *Energy Efficiency*.

[77] Grant Thompson, *Building to Save Energy: Legal and Regulatory Approaches* (New York, Ballinger, forthcoming).

[78] Letter from Blair T. Bower to Frederick R. Anderson, June 25, 1976.

[79] Letter from Dale L. Keyes to Frederick R. Anderson, May 19, 1976. Letter from Laurence I. Moss to Frederick R. Anderson, May 11, 1976.

[80] Dewees, "Travel, Cost, Transit," p. 73.

Hazardous and Toxic Substances

Charges and similar systems have been proposed and used to help control hazardous and toxic substances, but only to a limited extent. It can be argued that the dangers inherent in even small ongoing discharges or occasional larger spills of these substances are so great that legal prohibitions backed up with heavy penalties are the best control measures. However, charges can play a constructive role by providing an easily activated incentive for care in handling such substances and in placing the burden of cleaning up spills and paying for damages on those responsible.

The Japanese Compensation Law

The Japanese compensation law, discussed in detail in the section on air pollution, taxes dischargers of certain toxic substances and other pollutants in order to finance compensation for victims of diseases and other health damage caused by the pollutants. The compensation law is probably the most significant use of the charges approach in the toxics area.

Civil Penalties for Spills of Hazardous Substances

The Federal Water Pollution Control Act provides for the use of civil penalties to help control discharges and spills of hazardous substances.[81] This provision has not as yet been implemented. The penalties are to be graduated on the basis of the seriousness of resulting environmental harm. Penalties are to vary according to the toxicity, degradability, and dispersal characteristics of the substances. The EPA has proposed penalty amounts that would take these factors into account and has shown an interest in making the penalties large enough to make it economically wise to use care in handling hazardous substances and to act quickly to minimize damage when spills occur.[82] It should be noted that these penalties, like other civil penalty provisions discussed in this chapter, differ

[81] 33 U.S.C. §1321(b)(2)(ii), (iii), and (iv).
[82] EPA, "Determination of Units of Measurement & Rates of Penalty for Hazardous Substances, Notice of Proposed Rulemaking," *Federal Register* vol. 40 (1975), p. 59999.

basically from charges in two ways. First, they are paid after the fact, not regularly as a result of an ongoing activity. Thus the incentive stems from the potential for assessment, not the certainty of regular payments. Second, the penalties are not necessarily applied in every case. While they could be made automatic, such penalties are generally used selectively by enforcement officials on particular types of cases. In contrast, charges apply to all who engage in the charged behavior.

Other Systems

There are a number of other schemes that use charges, taxes, or penalties to help internalize some costs of damage from hazardous substances. A number of states have the authority to levy fines for spills that result in fish kills.[83] Such programs could be structured to take the economic costs of the kills into account. Companies responsible for oil spills can be required to pay all or part of the costs of cleanup in some areas.[84] A tax on producers of toxic chemicals has been proposed.[85] A New York City tax on cigarettes based on their tar and nicotine content could be considered to be a toxic substance tax.[86] Finally, a system of charges on low levels of radioactive emissions from nuclear power plants has been proposed.[87] The concept is alarming because it seems to sanction extremely dangerous discharges. However, a radioactive emissions charge might be an effective response to noncritical levels of emissions. It would be an automatic sanction that could not be avoided with excuses or elaborate defenses and thus if large enough, would be a direct incentive to exercise care to avoid low levels of radioactive emissions.

[83] Letter from Blair T. Bower to Frederick R. Anderson, June 25, 1976.

[84] 33 U.S.C. §1321(f)(1)(2)(3).

[85] National Academy of Sciences, "Decisionmaking for Regulating Chemicals in the Environment" (1975) pp. 15–16, 220–228.

[86] William Drayton, "The Tar and Nicotine Tax: Pursuing Public Health through Tax Incentives," *Yale Law Journal* vol. 81 (1972) p. 1487.

[87] Richard Wilson, "Charging for Radioactive Emissions," *Science* vol. 190 (October 1975) p. 460.

4

The Monitoring Problem

This chapter is devoted to a brief treatment of the technological questions involved in the design of a charge system, principally the technology associated with the monitoring of the substance subject to a charge. The discussion will concentrate on air and water pollution because the technological problems of effluent and emissions charges are the most complex and least understood, and it is on the real or imagined technological difficulties in these areas that critics of charges most often focus.

In the design of a charge system, the first question that must be confronted is: On what is the charge to be levied? The answer, unfortunately, is considerably more complex than "on pollution," or "on environmentally harmful activity." A charge designed to improve water quality, for example, must take into account the fact that there is no single index of water pollution. Whether a substance discharged into a waterway "pollutes" depends on a number of factors, including the use to which the waterway is put, the location of the discharge, and the time of day or year. Similarly, a charge designed to encourage a reduction in solid waste would not necessarily be the same for all types of wastes. It might be less, for example, for segregated materials such as paper, glass, or ferrous metals—which can fairly easily be recycled, than for undifferentiated garbage—which is more costly to deal with. A charge might be used to reduce automotive air pollution, but in its present state the internal combustion engine produces several different classes of air pollutants. An effective charge, therefore, would have to take into account the fact that engine modifications intended to reduce one exhaust component may have the effect of increasing others.

Another pair of important considerations are the points in the production-consumption cycle at which the charge is levied, and the identity of the party initially responsible for its payment. A tax on sulfur, for example, might be imposed on mine owners at the mine mouth, or on purchasers at the time of sale. It might also be imposed on utilities at the time the coal is burned. Similarly, a charge designed to curb automotive air pollution might be imposed on the manufacturer when the car is sold. It might be imposed on the operator at an annual pollution check. It might even be applied to the purchase of gasoline at rates which vary with the amount of pollution the car is estimated to generate for each gallon of gasoline consumed. Taxes to influence land development might be imposed on holding land, on the way it is used, on gains realized on its sale, on subdividing real property, and so on.

Once the parameter on which the charge is to be levied has been selected, the second technological problem is to devise an acceptably accurate and reliable means of measuring the parameter over time. In some cases this is simple to do, but in others the problems of measurement are sufficiently difficult to exert a major influence on the design of the system and may in some instances determine the choice of the parameter that is to bear the charge.

Monitoring Systems

"Monitoring" for charges not related to air and water pollution does not ordinarily require complicated technology. Charges designed to improve land use patterns, for example, can be based on number of acres (or square feet) or gains realized on the sale of land. Energy-conserving charges might be levied on the horsepower or weight or average gasoline mileage of motor vehicles. Antilitter taxes have been imposed on a per bottle basis. None of these devices requires more than a bit of imagination on the part of policymakers.

Monitoring for air and water pollution, however, poses somewhat more difficult problems. There are a number of criteria by which a monitoring system should be judged. The ideal measurement device would be a small black box which could be affixed to the stack, outfall, plant gate, or landscape to be monitored and would continuously measure and record the level of each of the

parameters on which charges are to be levied, as well as the total volume of gases, liquids, or solids discharged, with an accuracy of plus or minus 0.001 percent. This little box would be extremely reliable, require virtually no maintenance, be impervious to tampering, and cost no more than ten dollars a year to purchase, install, and operate. Of course, no such wondrous machine exists either in reality or even as a glimmer in the eyes of the instrument manufacturers. This being the case, we are forced to seek less ideal, but nevertheless satisfactory, approaches to the monitoring problem.

The most effective method of measuring (or estimating) the quantity and quality of a discharge varies immensely with the nature of the discharge and the parameter or parameters on which the pollution charge is based. It is not difficult to weigh a truck carrying solid refuse through a plant gate. It is quite another thing, however, to measure the weight of sulfur oxides being emitted from a power plant stack. It is not difficult to monitor continuously, accurately, and inexpensively the temperature or the conductivity of the liquid effluent leaving a factory or treatment plant. It is a good deal more difficult to determine the biochemical oxygen demand of the same effluent. It is likely, therefore, that not only the instrumentation, but the entire approach to the monitoring problem will vary widely in any workable charge system.

Self-reporting

One of the first questions which must be answered in designing a monitoring scheme is whether the initial burden of making the quantitative and qualitative measurements on which the charges are to be based will lie on the discharger or on the charging authority. When one considers the expense and the practical difficulties of allocating the entire measurement task to the government, the answer comes rather easily. The bureaucratic burden that would result from exclusive reliance on monitoring carried out by the regulators would be enormous, but fortunately this is a problem that is easily avoided by requiring each major pollution source to monitor and report its own discharges. Moreover, equity and economic efficiency suggest that the costs of monitoring be

imposed on the sources of the problem rather than on the public at large.[1]

But would not self-reporting provide too great a temptation for underreporting? Is it realistic to expect industry to be completely honest in its measurements? What happens when the measurement device breaks down (either accidentally or with assistance) and produces no data about pollutants? The answers to these questions are not so difficult as they may seem. To begin with, there is a precedent for the viability of a self-reporting approach in the income tax system. While it cannot be denied that there is some income tax cheating, the majority of business tax returns are entirely honest; the amount of false reporting is not nearly great enough to threaten the viability of the system. The application of a self-reporting system to charges would require occasional verification by the authorities (analogous to income tax audits) and penalties for intentional misreporting, but such provisions are hardly novel to our legal system. They might be supplemented in the environmental field by provisions for "bounties" to private citizens who developed evidence leading to the exposure of a polluter for false reporting.

A self-reporting system might also be used to resolve the problem of what degree of monitoring precision should be required. Presumptions can be established that bias the system toward a higher rather than a lower charge where there is an uncertainty in the reported measurements. If the discharger is permitted to overcome those presumptions by installing better monitoring equipment, each firm will be able to make its own tradeoff between using frequent measurements and more precise equipment, thus possibly lowering the charges it must pay, and relying on less reliable techniques or simple estimates and perhaps paying a higher charge.

Measuring Air and Water Pollution

Whether the responsibility for monitoring rests on the discharger or the charging authority, someone, at some time, will have to

[1] This self-reporting approach has survived constitutional challenges in at least one state.

measure the quantity of the discharges and the level of each of the parameters on which a charge is to be levied. There are a number of basic approaches which can be used in performing this function. Which one is most appropriate for a particular situation depends on the type of discharge, the parameter being measured, and the available monitoring technology. Most of the following discussion is devoted to the problems posed by the monitoring that would be required for charges aimed at air and water pollution. Little attention is directed at other uses of charges simply because, for the most part, monitoring in other areas can be accomplished without technological difficulty.

Water Pollution

FLOW RATE. The first problem to be faced in measuring discharges into either the air or the water is the measurement of the total rate of flow of the emissions or effluent that carries the pollutants. Most existing monitoring instruments do not measure quantities of a given pollutant, but only its concentration, or the level of some other parameter related to the environmental degradation resulting from the discharge. It is necessary then to measure the overall rate of discharge or at least some surrogate which will provide a reasonably accurate estimate. Flow measurement of liquid effluent is, for the most part, easy and inexpensive. There are any number of simple instruments and techniques for direct measurement of the flow of liquids, including venturimeters, rotameters, calibrated pumps, and weirs. These instruments are reliable, generally accurate enough for the need, and elementary to operate.

Just as easy is the technique of proportional sampling, in which periodic samples of the discharge are taken which are directly proportional in volume to the flow rate of the discharge at the time of sampling. These samples are combined into a composite sample which is representative of the average concentration of the substance or parameter of interest and of the average rate at which it was being discharged over the period during which the samples were drawn. Once drawn, this composite sample may be analyzed at a laboratory maintained by the plant, or at an unrelated private laboratory if the facility being sampled is too small to afford its own lab. The costs of a daily analysis of one of these composite

samples for the three or four parameters subject to a charge (e.g., BOD, suspended solids, and dissolved solids) would be easily within the means of all but the smallest dischargers. And it is possible that weekly or even monthly analysis would suffice for the majority of facilities.

Measuring the flow rate of the carrier liquid is but the first and easiest part of determining the quantity of pollutants actually being released by a plant to the environment. Far more complicated is the process of measuring the concentration or level of each of the substances or qualities on which a charge is to be levied.

CONCENTRATION. A natural body of water is, in a very real sense, alive. The complexity of the physical, biological, and chemical interactions that take place in a flowing stream is so great that we are still far from understanding or being able to describe completely even a substantial fraction of it. Each stream, river, lake, and estuary has unique flow patterns, temperature, salinity, pH (acidity), turbidity, inputs, and a myriad of other physical, biological, and chemical characteristics, which distinguish it and the life it supports from other bodies of water. The variation of conditions from one body of water to another and within one watercourse means that both the effect of a pollutant on a body of water and the effect of the water on the pollutant vary widely according to the conditions at the point of discharge and downstream. For example, the rate at which biological material is oxidized by the action of the biota in a stream depends on the temperature, the type of biota present and their condition, the pH of the water, the amount and type of suspended solids, and a host of other factors.

Although we still do not fully understand all of the complexities involved, it is possible nevertheless to make a number of generalizations about those characteristics of a watercourse which are most important to an understanding of the monitoring problem. There are some cases where other characteristics may be more important, but if only one variable were to be selected as an indicator of the health of a stream, it would certainly be the dissolved oxygen content. Usually measured in parts per million, dissolved oxygen may vary from about 8.4 parts per million (ppm), the saturation level at 25° C, to zero, a condition which indicates highly polluted waters. The minimum dissolved oxygen content for the support of

most fish life is about 5 ppm, although some fish, such as carp, can live with concentrations down to 4 ppm. When a stream is overloaded with oxygen-demanding material to the point that all of the dissolved oxygen is used up, decomposition of organic matter begins to take place anaerobically, an odorous process commonly associated by the average citizen with "water pollution." Extremely low levels of dissolved oxygen may also alter the nature of the flora and fauna in the waterway, sometimes with unaesthetic results.

Oxygen is restored to natural waters principally by the dissolution of atmospheric oxygen and by photosynthesis. The rates at which these processes occur vary markedly according to the amount of dissolved oxygen already present, the stream's geometry (the number of waterfalls and rapids, the width of the stream, etc.), the amount of sunlight and nutrients, the type of aquatic plant life, the temperature, and other factors. Since part of the process involves the activity of natural microorganisms, conditions affecting their health and numbers are also important, most notably the presence or absence of toxic materials.

The principal effect of most pollutants on stream quality is the reduction of dissolved oxygen caused by the biochemical oxidation of organic matter. Although it is not completely satisfactory, the best and most frequently used measure of the extent of the resulting oxygen demands is the pollutant's biochemical oxygen demand (usually abbreviated BOD).

Unfortunately, the only way to measure BOD is to observe the reduction of dissolved oxygen in a sample of the pollutant (which has been mixed with a standard culture of microbial oxidizing agents) after a period of several days. (The standard test lasts 5 days, and the oxygen demand thus determined is properly indicated as BOD_5.) Even when the tests are conducted under carefully controlled conditions in the laboratory, the resulting measurement of BOD is not generally considered to be very accurate. Obviously, such a test is not well suited for our ideal, on-site, direct-reading monitor. It is possible, however, to monitor continuously both total organic carbon (TOC) and chemical oxygen demand (COD), two other variables which are closely related to BOD and on which, under certain conditions, it may be possible to base a charge. The instruments for measuring these two quantities are relatively complicated and expensive but they can be adapted for

use in the field and are capable of producing a continuous record of the level of TOC or COD at the outfall. They currently bear price tags of $5,000 to $10,000 and require a fair amount of maintenance. But if the market for such instruments increased, they could probably be made less expensive and more reliable, and their use for a charge system is an entirely realistic possibility, at least for larger industrial and municipal dischargers.

A second important parameter of water quality is the amount of suspended solids in the stream. These small, often microscopic particles have varied effects on a stream's metabolism. They reduce the amount of light available for plant growth, they may serve as sites for bacterial activity, they can adsorb some substances and transport them downstream or carry them to the bottom as sediment, and they may have other effects which are even less well understood.

The most accurate means of measuring suspended solids is again sampling and laboratory analysis, although the laboratory work is quite simple and can be performed without the 5-day delay usually involved in the measurement of BOD. It is, however, possible to measure turbidity, which is in many cases a satisfactory surrogate for suspended solids, with a direct-reading, continuous monitor. Although turbidimeters tend to clog or cloud up, and the amount of light transmitted by the effluent may be reduced by causes other than suspended solids, with proper maintenance they are satisfactory for most applications and are relatively inexpensive.

There are many other characteristics of effluents which may have an impact on water quality, such as phosphorus and nitrogen content, although none are generally as important as BOD and suspended solids. Some of these parameters may be measured directly with quite simple instruments, for example, temperature, conductance (which is related to the concentration of dissolved solids), and pH (hydrogen ion concentration) are all easily and inexpensively monitored.

It is also possible to monitor continuously most inorganic and many organic compounds by using instruments which perform what amounts essentially to an automated laboratory analysis based on colorimetric (wet chemical), spectrographic, or other analytic techniques. These instruments are expensive ($5,000 to $15,000) and complex. They are also basically laboratory instruments which

tend to be somewhat delicate and may not withstand very well the rugged environment of an industrial plant. They are nevertheless available now, and it is feasible to use them to monitor the effluents of larger facilities where more precise continuous measurement of certain chemicals is necessary.

Air Pollution

FLOW RATE. The air pollutants which are presently of the greatest concern may be grouped into five classes: carbon monoxide, hydrocarbons, oxides of nitrogen, sulfur oxides, and particulates. There are also a number of hazardous substances such as asbestos, pesticides, beryllium, and mercury that constitute potential and in some cases actual hazards.

Measuring the flow of gases carrying air pollutants is somewhat more difficult than measuring the flow rate of a liquid effluent. To calculate the flow rate of a liquid in a pipe to the degree of accuracy with which we are concerned, it is necessary to know only the area of the pipe and the velocity at which the liquid is flowing. To measure the flow rate of gases in a stack, however, it is necessary to know not just area and velocity, but the pressure and the temperature of the gas as well. To complicate the picture even further, while for all practical purposes liquids flowing in an outfall can be treated as moving at the same velocity everywhere in the cross section of the pipe, the velocity of a gas in a stack often fluctuates widely from one part of the stack to another, as may its temperature and pressure. As a result, in the present state of measurement technology it is generally necessary to determine the velocity, temperature, and pressure at numerous points in the stack's cross section to arrive at a reasonably accurate estimate of the total flow rate.

The principal and currently most accurate means of making these measurements involves the insertion of a probe composed of a pitot tube (a device which measures velocity from the differential between the "dynamic pressure" and the "static" pressure of a moving gas) and a thermometer into the stack and "traversing" it so as to determine the temperature, pressure, and velocity at several points in the stack's cross section. One problem with this method is that, particularly in especially dirty stacks, the probes

often become clogged or fouled and give no reading or, worse, false readings. It is also fairly expensive to make a series of such readings because it occupies several technicians for a period of hours. Fortunately in many cases where the flow rate, temperature, and pressure do not fluctuate rapidly—as, for example, in most power plants—it is often possible to "calibrate" the stack so that a reasonable approximation of the flow rate may be calculated from one measurement taken at a known point in the stack. This obviously simplifies matters substantially and would even permit the production of a continuous record of flow rate.

There are also some other simpler techniques which may be adapted to flow measurement in a few cases where the flow patterns are simple and the velocity relatively low. These include the use of various types of anemometers, measurements of temperature differentials, and even the injection of colored smoke into the stack. But until the technology advances somewhat, it is likely that we will be forced to rely on the use of probes and sampling techniques for many applications, an approach that, while workable, leaves something to be desired in terms of cost, convenience, and accuracy.

CONCENTRATION. Measurement of the concentration of the important air pollutants as they leave a source also provides a somewhat greater technological challenge than direct monitoring of water pollutants. Virtually the only method of monitoring now in widespread use requires inserting a probe in the stack to be tested and withdrawing samples which are then analyzed by filtering out and weighing the particulate matter and then using standard wet chemical, or more sophisticated photometric, spectrographic, chemiluminescent chromatographic, or coulometric techniques to measure the gaseous components. Presently most such testing is done manually and on only an infrequent basis, and it presents many of the same practical problems as the determination of flow rates. Conditions vary from place to place within the cross section of the stack, and, in many industrial processes, fluctuate sharply, depending on the state of the production cycle. Probes clog easily. Samples must be withdrawn isokinetically (i.e., a vacuum must be maintained on the probe so that the velocity of the gases entering the probe matches that of the gases moving up the stack). The

state of the materials in the stack gases, whether solid, liquid or gas, depends on the temperature of the gases, and a change of temperature of the sample during its analysis may affect the results. In short, at the present state of the art, stack gas sampling and analysis are difficult and often imprecise. Nevertheless, with permanently installed probes and sample handling equipment, and using one of the more technically sophisticated instruments for measuring the concentration of the various gases in the sample, it is presently possible to monitor continuously any of the gaseous pollutants of greatest concern. The available detection instruments currently cost on the order of $5,000 to $10,000, and two or three may be required for some applications. Another $5,000 to $10,000 would appear to be a reasonable estimate of the cost of installing a probe and sample handling equipment, bringing the total capital cost of each installation up to $10,000 to $50,000 dollars, depending on the needs and configuration of the plant, with the average being probably located toward the low end of that scale.

New and potentially more accurate and less costly techniques of stack gas monitoring are also on the horizon. A large amount of federal and private money is being spent on the development of new instruments which would overcome many of the problems of sampling and sample handling. Some of the more promising methods involve taking advantage of the selectivity of the interaction of gas molecules and light energy from certain portions of the electromagnetic spectrum. Laser techniques have already been used to identify some gases at the mouth of a stack. There are now commercially available SO_2/NO_x monitors available for power plants which can achieve a $\pm$ 10 percent accuracy and cost between $10,000 and $15,000. For an additional $5,000 or so it is possible to purchase an instrument which is accurate to within 5 percent. It is only a matter of time before even more accurate instruments come on the market.

At this point very little progress has been made on satisfactory techniques for the continuous monitoring of particulates, which remains a particularly intractable problem. But it appears that within five years it should be possible to monitor directly and continuously most of the relatively few gases which pose significant air pollution problems at costs which are acceptable for all except the smallest emitters. Moreover, technological advances in the moni-

toring field would be spurred considerably by the institution of charge systems since they would create an incentive for research on instrumentation.

Direct, continuous monitoring of emissions or effluents may be feasible for larger installations where suitable instruments are available, and their cost is small relative to the overall cost of operating the plant. But as we have seen, instrument technology does not provide solutions for every monitoring problem. Such instruments as are available may carry price tags too large for the budget of the small discharger, and they are useful only for point sources. Some other technique would have to be applied for pollution from feed lots, acid mine runoff, dust-generating cement plants, and other sources whose wastes do not go up a stack or out a pipe. Were continuous monitoring essential to the success of a charge system, this technological gap would pose a problem to the implementation of a pollution charge for such industries. But fortunately some approach less ideal than direct monitoring may in many cases serve quite satisfactorily.

Alternative Monitoring Methods

Sampling

One relatively simple approach to monitoring pollutants that has been used with success is the proportional sampling and laboratory analysis procedure outlined on page 94. Some dischargers who wished to adopt this approach for water pollutants would meet problems arising out of a multiplicity of outfalls. Particularly in the case of older plants, even the plant engineers often do not even know the location of all of the outfalls. Combining a large number of waste-carrying pipes into one—or at least a small number of outfalls—the contents of which could be sampled, would no doubt involve substantial expenditures in some cases. But here, as in the case of most of the other anticharge arguments based on alleged difficulties of monitoring, the problem is no more difficult than it would be for any other effective pollution abatement system. Any workable approach to the reduction of pollution must include some means of controlling and measuring what is discharged, and

to achieve that it is necessary to know what is being discharged—from all outfalls.

Sampling and laboratory analysis as an approach to measuring gaseous emissions is somewhat more difficult. To begin with, drawing samples of gases from a stack is harder than drawing samples of liquid from an outfall. On top of that, gaseous samples, once collected, are far more difficult to handle than a container of liquid effluent, and the constituents of stack gas tend to be unstable and sensitive to changes in temperature and pressure. Where the sampling problems can be overcome, however, it is not beyond the realm of possibility that in cases where frequent sampling is necessary or desirable, smaller plants might find it easier and cheaper to draw periodic samples of their stack gases and send them to commercial laboratories than to maintain the fairly elaborate equipment currently necessary to perform adequate analyses.

Materials Balance

It is extremely important that discussion of the technical problems of end-of-pipe or top-of-stack measurements not mislead us into focusing exclusively on that one particular approach to monitoring. There are other ways to determine the levels of discharges besides direct measurement, and in many cases they are far superior. One of the most useful of these alternative approaches to "monitoring" certain types of discharge is the materials balance. When it is possible to measure fairly accurately the quantities of both the inputs and outputs of a process, the difference, if any, may be assumed to be residuals discharged to the environment via effluent or emissions. For the simpler industrial process, it is relatively easy to perform the measurements and calculations necessary to determine the nature and amount of any discharges. The materials balance approach is already in widespread use in water quality management as a method for measuring the quantity of sewage discharged to municipal treatment plants in order to establish the sewer fees to be paid by industrial dischargers.

Another frequently mentioned application of the materials balance technique is the determination of the amount of sulfur oxides emitted by a power plant. It is a simple matter to determine by chemical analysis the sulfur content of a fuel, and since virtually

all of the sulfur is burned in the combustion process, it may be safely assumed that, without stack gas treatment, it all goes up the stack in the form of sulfur oxides. If a plant installs abatement equipment to remove sulfur from the stack gases, it is again a relatively simple matter to determine the amount removed and deduct that from the total sulfur burned to arrive at the amount that goes up the stack.

Of course, not all industrial processes are as simple as the combustion of coal or oil in a power plant. And charge systems will require quantitative measurements of much greater complexity than the determination of the volume of effluent discharged into a sewer system. The materials balance is obviously not adaptable to all discharge monitoring problems, but it is one relatively inexpensive technique that can be used to good effect in a large variety of applications. In some of these applications it may be even more accurate and reliable than any presently available direct measurement techniques.

Estimation

Where satisfactory techniques for actually measuring discharges, either directly or indirectly, are unavailable, or where the available techniques impose expenses that are unduly burdensome in relation to the size of the enterprise being monitored, it may be necessary to simply estimate the quantities in question. There are probably many cases in which the degree of accuracy achieved by estimation would be satisfactory to both the charging authority and the discharger; and it may be used in preference to direct measurement even where relatively inexpensive direct monitoring techniques are available. For example, the Ruhr basin water associations discussed in chapter 3 limit their monitoring to a periodic sampling and fairly crude laboratory analysis of a discharger's effluent. The samples are taken only infrequently from any given plant; and in practice many, if not most, of the dischargers are satisfied to pay fees based on estimates of the quantity and strength of their discharges derived from various measures of plant activity.

Estimation may also be the only feasible monitoring procedure in the case of very small dischargers, such as automobiles or domes-

tic oil burners, or in the case of nonpoint sources such as feedlots or strip mines. Estimates may frequently be tied to some measure of the activity of a discharger. In the Czechoslovakian system discussed in chapter 3, for example, the amount of BOD discharged by a brewery is estimated according to a formula which includes the number of employees (to take into account the use of sanitary facilities), the number of kegs and returnable bottles washed, the number of kegs and bottles filled (to take into account spillage), and the total quantity of beer produced. Coefficients for each of these parameters have been developed empirically and are applied uniformly to all breweries. Any individual plant has the option to demonstrate that process changes or treatment facilities have reduced the amount of BOD in its effluent below the estimated value and thereby receive a reduction in the charges payable. It should be possible in most cases to develop a set of parameters and coefficients like these which will enable the charging authority to estimate the quantities of air or water pollutants discharged by a given plant using a given production method with a fair degree of accuracy.

Estimation is probably best used in conjunction with other techniques, principally sampling, which can serve to augment and verify the figures developed by estimation. It may in fact be the most attractive of all the monitoring techniques. First, once the estimation formulas have been developed, applying them to determine the amount of the charge due is virtually costless. And so long as the formulas are reasonably accurate, the estimation approach would not be subject to challenge as being arbitrary. If, as would usually be the case, the discharger may reduce the charges payable by demonstrating that its discharges are less than the estimates, the discharger is free to make the economic choice between potential savings on charges and the expense of installing monitoring equipment which would produce a more accurate, and presumably lower, indication of the quantities being discharged. The same economic principles will operate to provide a badly needed incentive for the development of new, less expensive, and more accurate monitoring instruments. Thus estimation as a "monitoring" technique partakes of many of the same economic advantages which make pollution charges themselves so attractive.

Summary

Much of the criticism of environmental charges has revolved around the assertion that, when applied to air and water problems at least, measuring the emissions or effluent produced by every source subject to charges will be too difficult or expensive to be practicable. The simplest response to this argument is that it over-looks the fact that *any* effective pollution control system will require some means of monitoring and assessing the environmental harm done or the quantity of pollutants discharged from each major source (e.g., industrial plants and treatment facilities) and at least a sampling of minor sources (e.g., automobiles and house-holds).

The design of charge systems will necessarily be influenced to at least some extent by what it is technically and economically feasible to measure. It appears likely that research and development now in progress will soon produce more rugged, more reliable, and less expensive monitoring equipment; but even if it does not, or if the improvements in the near future are only marginal, continuous instrumental monitoring of most of the parameters to which we might desire to attach a charge is already technically feasible, and, for larger plants at any rate, is economically within the realm of the possible as well.

On the other hand, monitoring difficulties might be a disadvantage of a charge system relative to other approaches if the use of charges were to require more precise or detailed information than, for example, a conventional regulatory approach. The charging authority must strike a balance between the benefits accruing from more accurate and reliable measurement of the parameter on which a charge is to be levied and the costs of purchasing, operating, and maintaining the more expensive equipment necessary to achieve increased accuracy and reliability. The level at which this balance will be struck could vary widely from industry to industry and region to region. In many cases, the level of accuracy satisfactory for the purposes of an environmental charge will likely be no higher than that which would be required for an effective system of administrative regulation. In some instances it may even be less. Wherever this is true, the "monitoring problem" disappears as a

relevant consideration in evaluating the feasibility of a charge system.

Obviously, the results of applying a charge at different points and on different users and of basing its amount on varying measures of activity or of value will have differing incentive effects, some of which will conform more closely to a desired policy outcome than others. The point is that, with imagination and careful analysis, charges can be used with great effect to solve a wide range of environmental problems.

5

The Law of Charges

Proposals for environmental charges are shaped by the law no less than by the natural environment, economic behavior, technology, and politics. The draftsman who prepares the proposal, the legislator who votes on it, the administrator who implements it, and the judge who reviews its lawfulness are all influenced by their perceptions of legal issues. Although each of these persons approaches charges from a different perspective, he must take account of the impact of the plan upon individual liberties, private property rights, the allocation of power between the federal and state governments, and the separation between legislative, judicial, and executive functions.

We have no doubt that Congress and the state legislatures have the constitutional power to enact charges plans. The sources of the power and restraints on its exercise do, however, need to be explored with care, because legal constraints channel the formation of charges plans, even if they do not block their creation. The difficulty comes in basing a new concept like charges upon traditional legal powers and in reconciling it with traditional legal protections. A resolution of these difficulties is attempted in this chapter.

Legislative Powers and Charges

The Power of Congress: The Commerce Clause

The federal government still is, in theory at least, a government of limited authority. The states retain all legislative power not specif-

ically conferred on Congress by the Constitution. During a century and a half of national growth, however, the courts have gradually reversed the balance of power between the federal and the state governments. That shift occurred in large part through the courts' expansive reading of the commerce clause, which grants Congress the power "to regulate commerce . . . among the several States." Lacking other constitutional language that was as conveniently flexible, the courts have turned to the commerce clause to sustain all manner of federal regulation, and environmental regulation is no exception. The states retain their traditional powers over commerce, health and safety—but, backed by the courts, Congress has steadily enlarged the federal role in environmental protection through increasing reliance upon the commerce power.

Congress pointed out the effect of poor air quality on interstate commerce in enacting the Clean Air Act. The text of the Act states that air pollution results in danger to public health, injury to agriculture and livestock, damage to property, and hazard to air and ground transportation.[1] Pursuing a variation of the same approach, one district court has held that because ambient air moves across state lines, emitted particles may themselves be viewed as part of commerce and subjected to direct regulation.[2] Congress has also relied on the commerce clause in regulating pesticides, noise, solid waste, and other environmental pollutants. Some persons have urged that the federal power be used to control environmental problems even more subject to the traditional exercise of local power than air and water, that is, land use and fish and game control.[3] Finally, the federal commerce power extends to states and municipalities, whose polluting activities can be regulated as completely as if they were private corporations.[4]

The commerce power has been invoked to deal with such an array of social and environmental problems that almost any imag-

[1] The statutory language appears in 42 U.S.C. §1857 (a)(2) (1970).

[2] *United States* v. *Bishop Processing Co.*, 287 F. Supp. 624, 629 (D. Md. 1968), aff'd 423 F.2d 469 4th Cir. (1970), cert. denied 398 U.S. 904 (1970).

[3] Philip Sopher, "The Constitutional Framework," in Erica Dolgin and Thomas Guilbert, eds., *Federal Environmental Law* (St. Paul, Minn., West Publishing, 1974) pp. 33–39.

[4] Silas Lyman, "The Constitutionality of Effluent Charges," pp. 140–156. (Master of Laws thesis, University of Wisconsin School of Law, 1969. Available from the Clearinghouse for Federal Scientific and Technical Information, Springfield, Va. 22151 PB 190 667.)

inable and reasonable strategy for control resting upon it is likely to survive judicial challenge. Enhanced public understanding of complex environmental interrelationships almost guarantees a scientifically correct escape from constitutional limitations on the exercise of legislative power. If the first law of ecology is valid and all things are demonstrably interrelated, then the distinction between interstate and intrastate activities loses its force. Moreover, economic factors follow the requirements of nature and are likely to be just as far reaching as the ecological interconnections. Congress and the courts have relied on relationships much more tenuous than those readily available in the environmental area to establish the federal power to legislate. Congress may choose not to exercise its powers fully, out of political deference to local control on historical or policy grounds, but the constitutional barriers have long since fallen.

The characteristics of charges plans present no particular problems for the application of the commerce power. Like existing regulatory legislation, they would protect health, life, foodstuffs, and property; would protect and encourage interstate commerce and its channels and instrumentalities; and would prevent the spread of harmful substances among states. In particular, charges would use the existing market mechanisms of interstate commerce to achieve a more efficient and equitable allocation of resources among competing uses. Assuming that charges achieve what is claimed for them, they are not significantly different in the constitutional perspective from the wide array of policy implements already based on the commerce power.

Police Power of the States

The state legislatures have had the power to enact environmental regulatory programs for much longer than has the Congress. Their traditional "police power" includes the residual (and overlapping) power over commerce, which is not negligible, and the power to safeguard local health and welfare. Through the police power, the states had the first opportunity to improve the quality of the environment. That they did not all willingly undertake that task until required to do so under new federal–state programs can be explained by political reluctance, not legal disability. The power

was always there, and in some states it is now undergoing a tardy rebirth.

A long series of Supreme Court cases affirms in expansive rhetoric that the police power extends to all aspects of social welfare—not only to health, morals, and safety, but to the well-being, spaciousness, tranquility, and aesthetic appearance of a community as well. Thus the police power extends to virtually all forms of environmental protection. The Court has sustained public nuisance statutes, litter ordinances, zoning, and even protection of the purely aesthetic qualities of the local environment. The Supreme Court has said that air pollution "clearly falls within the exercise of even the most traditional concept of what is compendiously known as the police power."[5]

Charges plans present no more problems for the exercise of the police power than they do for the federal commerce power. The Supreme Court of Oregon, for example, had no difficulty in upholding the constitutionality of the state's first charges scheme—a charge on returnable beverage containers, enacted in conjunction with a ban on nonreturnable containers—as a valid exercise of Oregon's police power.[6]

Because the police power is broad, its exercise may conflict with the federal guarantee of free interstate commerce. In a federal system overlaying nationwide markets, local measures may fetter the larger national market system with parochial economic restraints that the courts will invalidate. Conflict between state charges schemes and federal protection of commerce could scuttle a state plan. Charges are just as vulnerable as any other form of state regulation that affects interstate commerce. Because this potential barrier to some types of plans could become important if a judicial challenge is mounted, it will be discussed later in this chapter in the section on legal constraints on charges plans.

The Tax Power—An Additional Basis?

Congress and the state legislatures, we need hardly be reminded, have the constitutional power to levy and collect taxes. The primary purpose of taxation is to raise the revenue necessary to meet

---

[5] *Huron Cement Co.* v. *Detroit*, 362 U.S. 440, 442 (1960).

[6] *American Can Co.* v. *Oregon Liquor Control Commission*, 517 F. 2d 691, *Environmental Law Reporter* vol. 4, p. 20218. (Ct. App. Ore. 1973.)

the expenses of government. In deciding what to tax and how heavily to tax it, however, legislators have often sought other objectives along with revenue gathering. Among these objectives is providing an economic disincentive to engage in environmentally undesirable behavior. A tax computed in the same way one computes a charge on environmentally undesirable substances and behavior also provides an economic disincentive.

Whether or not it is good policy, and lively debate has taken place on the wisdom of making nonrevenue-generating uses of the tax system, the federal and state tax laws are already used to pursue a variety of social objectives. The Supreme Court has specifically upheld regulatory taxes on drugs, firearms, and gambling. Federal and state cigarette and alcohol taxes appear to be set as much to discourage consumption as to gather revenue. The Internal Revenue Code permits taxpayers to amortize their investments in pollution control facilities much more rapidly than they may those in other facilities. The tax laws of at least 31 states include similar provisions.[7]

As we have already seen in chapter 3, the state of Vermont has relied upon the tax power in enacting a rather sophisticated land gains tax to discourage speculative subdivision and resale of farmland. Vermont has thus provided an economic disincentive against the rapid conversion of its rural countryside into small lots for vacation homes, and has slowed the consequent population increase and change in life-style. Revenue was decidedly a secondary consideration.

A tax on nicotine and tar in cigarettes, imposed by New York City in mid-1971, was specifically intended to discourage smoking and to cause a shift from the more toxic brands to less toxic ones. Imposed on top of the flat 4¢-a-pack general cigarette tax, the special tax has apparently caused a shift from taxed to exempt brands of 12–13 percent of all cigarettes sold in the city. Cigarette smoking continues, but smokers are switching to less highly "polluting" brands.[8]

The courts have been tolerant of the use of taxation as a means for carrying out a regulatory plan. In the *Sunshine Coal* case, the

[7] Comment, "Tax Incentives to Combat Pollution," *Journal of Urban Law* vol. 50, (1972) p. 273.

[8] William Drayton, "The Tar and Nicotine Tax: Pursuing Public Health through Tax Incentives," *Yale Law Journal* vol. 81 (1972) p. 1487.

Supreme Court was asked to examine a federal regulatory statute that discouraged the sale of coal at prices in excess of those developed under the statutory scheme. Discouragement was specifically provided by a tax amounting to almost one-fifth the price a producer might receive if he sold coal outside the plan. The Court rejected the contention that the tax was simply a penalty for refusing to accept the plan and hence was invalid as an exercise of the tax power, stating that although the tax was primarily a sanction to enforce the regulatory scheme, Congress could use the tax power to create a sanction for the exercise of its regulatory power.[9]

The *Sunshine Coal* case also raises the question whether Congress could rely upon the tax power to reach behavior that it could not reach under its other powers. One line of authority says that it cannot. The *Sunshine Coal* case itself is often cited for the proposition that if Congress otherwise has no power to regulate, but attempts to do so under the tax power, all provisions that are regulatory in nature, and extraneous to revenue gathering must be stricken.

Yet, in a later case the Supreme Court said precisely the opposite:

> It is beyond serious question that a tax does not cease to be valid merely because it regulates, discourages, or even definitely deters the activities taxed. . . . The principle applies even though the revenue obtained is obviously negligible . . . or the revenue purpose of the tax may be secondary. . . . Nor does a tax statute necessarily fall because it touches on activities which Congress might not otherwise regulate. As was pointed out in *Magnano Co.* v. *Hamilton,* 292 U.S. 40, 47 (1934): "From the beginning of our government, the courts have sustained taxes although imposed with the collateral intent of effecting ulterior ends which, considered apart, were beyond the Constitutional power of the lawmakers to realize by legislation directly addressed to their accomplishments."[10]

The Supreme Court appears to have reaffirmed this view recently, and the Supreme Court of Vermont said in its decision rejecting a challenge to the land gains tax that the legislature's power to achieve particular social and economic objectives by im-

9 *Sunshine Coal Co.* v. *Adkins,* 310 U.S. 381 (1940).

10 *United States* v. *Sanchez,* 340 U.S. 42, 44 (1950). See also *Sonzinsky* v. *United States,* 300 U.S. 506, 513–514 (1937).

posing a tax in a particular manner was "beyond question," even if the objectives were beyond those of the legislature's other powers.[11]

Hence, charges plans apparently can be enacted under the power to tax. No fundamental constitutional challenge to such a "tax" is likely to succeed. But exclusive reliance on the tax power does pose certain legal risks.

Exclusive reliance on the tax power can be easily avoided by the legislature, and were we confident that legislatures would either specify an open-ended array of powers which it felt was adequate, or simply say nothing, letting the courts identify the appropriate powers (as in some civil rights legislation), then it would not be necessary to point out the problems discussed here. The courts could be trusted to recognize that the commerce and police powers are preferable bases for charges, which are basically regulatory in nature and are not revenue-gathering measures. Yet some proponents of charges have found it convenient to speak of "pollution taxes" or "effluent taxes." They significantly underplay the regulatory aspects of such charges. Thus it may come about that a legislature rests its charges bill solely on the tax power. If it does so, and if the courts construe the plan as a tax, all or parts of it may be subject to legal constraints that could significantly alter its scope or even undercut its fundamental viability.

The first such constraint upon federal legislation is the constitutional requirement that an indirect tax, such as an excise tax, must be uniform. Nearly all states have similar constitutional provisions requiring uniformity and equality in taxation. These provisions might possibly be interpreted to require a much greater degree of uniformity in setting charges than would be optimal under the regulatory scheme. For example, it might be desirable to set a charge for biological oxygen demand at a higher level in one river basin than in another, reflecting different estimates of incentives effects. The issue then becomes whether the requirement of uniformity would prohibit this result.

The requirement should not impose a serious barrier, because taxes frequently have been sustained although different rates applied to subcategories of taxable activities and items, and although

[11] San Antonio School District v. Rodriquez, 411 U.S. 1 (1973); Andrews v. Lathrop, 315 A.2d 860 (Vt. Sup. Ct. 1973) Environmental Law Reporter vol. 4, p. 20571.

the tax was progressive. The test appears to be whether reasonable grounds exist for any classifications which are made. The mischief that the federal provision was designed to prevent is discrimination against a state; the state constitutional provisions prevent similar abuses locally. Such abuses can usually be cured, short of voiding every subclassification of a tax that results in different tax rates in different geographic locales.

The economic factors which argue for setting charges at different levels also provide the necessary legal justification for differentiated charges structures. Hence it appears to us that even an ideal, highly differentiated charge which varies according to substance, region, type of producer, time of day, assimiliative capacity, and the like could be sustained as "uniform" taxation, despite the wide differences in tax payments by polluters.

The second possible constraint on the exercise of the tax power concerns the application of federal charges plans to state and local governments. The law confers an immunity from federal taxation on state and municipal functions that have never been federally taxed, or were not federally taxed before state or local government took them over from private persons. The issue becomes important because the immunity protects municipal sewage treatment works from taxation as part of a federal wastewater effluent charges plan. The immunity cannot be claimed by a state or municipality that took over a function previously taxable under federal law when it was performed by private persons. But federal taxes have never been levied on wastewater discharges, nor upon most other environmentally damaging functions assumed, or likely to be assumed, by state or local governments.

A way around this immunity is suggested by the 1972 Federal Water Pollution Control Act Amendments, which require municipalities to collect user charges from private parties to help defray the cost of municipal treatment facilities. Although the charge is called a user fee, not a tax, there would be little difference if the federal law instructed the municipality to collect a "pollution tax." The major difference would come if the federal law also required the municipality to place the tax revenues in the federal treasury. Can Congress evade the tax immunity merely by making local government its agent for collection?

The answer appears to be yes, for the reason that the tax would not be paid by local government itself, but rather by private parties under a local tax scheme compelled by federal law. Ample authority exists for having state and local governments serve as federal tax collectors.

A challenge to a charge specifically enacted as a tax might be mounted on a third, rather novel ground. Federal and state constitutions require that all revenue bills originate in the popular chamber, which in the Congress is the House of Representatives. As unlikely as it may seem, a charge "tax" that did not originate in the lower house could conceivably be attacked as procedurally infirm, although we hasten to point out that the courts have been exceedingly reluctant to hold that the issue even is justiciable.[12]

The Supreme Court of Vermont has indicated that the infirmity applies, if at all, only to bills which "levy taxes in the strict sense of the word, whose primary purpose is to raise revenue. . . ."[13] Bills which generate revenue incident to other purposes are exempted. Such an interpretation does accord with the view that the federal constitutional provision originated in the conflict between the popularly elected English House of Commons and the Crown-dominated House of Lords and was included in the federal constitution to preserve direct popular control over taxation at a time when the Senate was elected by the state legislatures.

User Fees and Service Charges

Some advocates of charges have said that user fees present the closest analogy between a charges approach and the existing control strategy. However, charges act to change behavior and control pollution while returning to the public some compensation for damages that cannot be avoided. User fees, on the other hand, are generally viewed as a price to be paid for the use of public services and resources. Thus, while we agree that the analogy has instructional value, we think the legal implications of pursuing the analogy too far should be explored.

[12] *Rainey v. United States*, 232 U.S. 310 (1914); *Mikell v. Philadelphia School District*, 58 A.2d 339 (1948).
[13] *Andrews v. Lathrop*, 315 A.2d at 866.

State governments and their instrumentalities routinely impose user and service charges under the police power for the use of a public facility or a publicly managed resource. Examples include sewer charges, garbage collection fees, water rates, motor vehicle fuel taxes, park and beach use fees, and metered parking charges.

Local user and service charges do have chargelike side effects in that the public is being reimbursed for its investment or for the expense of maintaining the service or resource. In the case of sewer charges computed on the basis of the quantity and quality of the waste discharged, the analogy to effluent charges is quite close, particularly if the effluent charge were based on the estimated costs of abatement. Similarly, the ton-mile tax, levied by many states for the commercial use of highways, is based upon the extent and severity of usage.

Yet, the differences between the fees and charges concepts are on balance greater. The goal of the charges approach is abatement; of service and user fees, reimbursement for services rendered. Revenue is secondary under the charges approach, but it is primary under the user and service fees approach. User and service fees are typically computed on the basis of the costs to government of providing the service of policing the resource; economic charges are computed on the basis of social costs, the marginal incentive they will provide, or the cost of treatment. Finally, one might argue, but not conclusively, that the public does not "own" water, air, the aesthetic quality of a landscape, or tranquility in the same way it does sewerage, trash collection systems, parks, highways, and the like.

The question of ownership, in fact, presents interesting legal problems. A legislature considering a charges bill might not want to assert a property right, on the use of which a fee could be imposed, when conventional regulatory approaches avoid the controversy. In the case of effluent charges, the law weaves a tangled web concerning property rights. Navigable waters are apparently owned by the United States, and state waters are subject to a public trust; however, between private parties, waters are privately owned and subject to varying legal doctrines limiting the manner of use. The conventional regulatory perspective avoids the ownership issue.

If an economic charge is adopted that in fact is characterized as a user fee or service charge, it risks being invalidated because the

charge was more than reasonably necessary to carry out the service or protect the use, or because it really was a revenue measure and hence subject to the restrictions on taxation discussed above. The risk is real, but the general rule that fees and charges must bear some reasonable relationship to the costs of regulation, inspection, and control is undercut by a number of exceptions. Because of these exceptions, a charges plan would probably fare well in the courts, even if subjected to the case law on fees and charges. Most courts have held that if the activity on which the fee is levied could injure the public, fees may be set high enough to cause a cutback in the activity. A Minnesota court said that if a business had the potential of degenerating into a "nuisance," the police power could be exercised to impose a "license fee" large enough to "restrain" the offending behavior. An Illinois court allowed fees well in excess of regulatory costs where liquor license fees were challenged, as did a Washington state court faced with a challenge to a fee imposed on trading stamps.[14]

Fees which are directly applied to meet regulatory costs, maintain a public service, or replace used-up public resources more easily escape categorization as a tax. A plan that earmarked charges for environmental improvement would also enjoy this advantage. In a well-known case rejecting the view that the excess revenue from parking meters was illegal because it was far more than needed to meet the administrative costs of metering, the court relied on the city's use of the excess revenues for the limited purposes of maintaining overall traffic control and constructing additional parking facilities.[15] In a similar case the court sustained a $200 per lot fee where real estate developers did not provide adequate space for schools and parks in subdivisions. The fee was imposed so that the city could purchase the space not provided by the developer.[16]

These are rather good examples of a charge internalizing some social costs, deterring overload of city services, and providing a choice for the "polluter." In summing up the law on this point, a

---

[14] *Lyons* v. *City of Minneapolis*, 241 Minn. 439, 63 (1954); *Sager* v. *City of Silvis*, 402 Ill. 262 (1949) (liquor license fees); *Tanner* v. *Little*, 240 U.S. 369 (1915) (Washington trading stamps).

[15] *Skidmore* v. *City of Elizabethtown*, 291 S.W. 2d 3 (Ky. 1956).

[16] *Jordan* v. *Village of Menomonee Falls*, 28 Wisc. 2d 608 137 N.W. 2d 442 (1966).

leading authority on taxation almost lapsed into the economist's idiom. Cooley said that the direct expense of regulation and "all the incidental consequences that may be likely to subject the public to cost in consequence of the business licensed" could be included in the fees. He goes on to say that these costs may even be the reason the fee was originally set.[17]

Environmental charges, then, may possibly be sustained as user charges under existing case law. However, the limitations on the fee concept suggest avoiding this designation and resting the charges approach on its unique aspects. Earmarking charges income, for example, may be undesirable. Under the charges approach, there is no reason to spend the incidental income on environmental control. Legal safeguards against abuse of the police power in levying money fees, as they appear in the cases above, must be heeded. The constitutional bases of these safeguards will be discussed in the next section.

Legal Constraints on Charges Plans

Each power of government is coupled with restraints on its abuse. Limits on the exercise of the commerce, police, and tax powers will be discussed in this section. None of these constraints bars the charges approach, but each does affect the scope and design of particular plans. Federal and state constitutional guarantees such as due process and the equal protection of law, the federal preemption of certain fields of regulation, and the separation of legislative, executive, and judicial functions must all be heeded in carrying out the charges strategy.

Analogies between charges and other environmental control techniques again play an important role. The courts will be tempted to categorize charges as taxes, fines, fees, or the like, and to burden them with the safeguards against abuse associated with them. Up to the point when the analogy breaks down, the application of these safeguards is entirely appropriate. But beyond, the unique nature of the charges approach may make application of safeguards inappropriate. Without mischief to remedy, the "safe-

---

[17] Clark A. Nichols, ed., *Law of Taxation* vol. 4 (Chicago, Callahan) §1809, p. 3555.

guards" may hamper the functioning of the charges approach without a corresponding public gain.

Due Process and Equal Protection

The due process and equal protection clauses of federal and state constitutions guarantee the basic reasonableness and fairness of any legislative scheme. "Due process of law" has many guises. It includes general due process in legislative programs, "substantive" due process in the particular content of the legislative program itself, the prohibition against taking of property without due process and compensation, and "criminal" due process where penalties are levied. The similar safeguard of "equal protection of law" bars discriminatory interference in private affairs which may be caused by arbitrary legislative classifications. Particularly important are the safeguards accorded the criminally accused, because courts may conclude that some charges plans are in fact money penalties, the imposition of which requires provision of the constitutionally mandated procedural and other safeguards of the criminal law.

The Fifth and Fourteenth amendments guarantee that federal and state governments will meet basic requirements of fairness when they enact and administer regulatory programs. State constitutions contain similar provisions.

> The Fifth Amendment, in the field of federal activity, and the Fourteenth, as respects state action, do not prohibit governmental regulation for the public welfare. They merely condition the exertion of the admitted power by securing that the end shall be accomplished by methods consistent with due process. And the guaranty of due process, as has often been held, demands only that the law shall not be unreasonable, arbitrary or capricious, and that the means selected shall have a real and substantial relation to the object sought to be attained.[18]

Any well-designed charges plan should be able to meet the requirement that it be reasonably related to the purpose of environmental control, especially since the courts are unlikely to undercut the legislature's judgment unless the proposal entirely lacks a rational basis. The economic rationale for environmental charges, as developed in chapter 2, is at least as rational as the strategies

[18] *Nebbia* v. *New York*, 291 U.S. 502, 525 (1933).

currently pursued, for which due process challenges have never been seriously entertained. Unless particular charges schemes are developed in an unreasonable or arbitrary manner, they will easily meet these minimal due process requirements.

The equal protection clause of the Fourteenth Amendment, as interpreted in the courts, provides that the states may not enact legislation which discriminates unfairly against certain classes of persons, nor may a statute, fair on its face, be administered in a discriminatory fashion. The Fifth Amendment, coupled by judicial interpretation with the Fourteenth, forbids Congress to do the same. State constitutions contain provisions that have been similarly interpreted. Although equal protection (and sometimes due process) has most often been invoked to protect individuals against discriminatory classifications based on race, religion, and sex, it applies to corporations as well as human beings.

The courts test a statutory classification against the equal protection standard by asking whether the statutory categories are based on differences that are "reasonably related" to the purposes for which the statute was enacted. Obviously, this judge-made standard is very imprecise. One needs to look at how specific cases were decided to get a better idea of the strength of the prohibition as it might be applied to environmental charges. The question is important because charges plans ordinarily will establish many different levels and categories of charge, to permit maximum reliance upon the incentive effect.

The Supreme Court has voided very few state measures except where discrimination based on race or nationality has been shown. The Court has itself characterized the equal protection clause as the "usual last resort of constitutional argument."[19] Maryland's highest court has expressed the kind of judicial reception a challenge to charges would probably be accorded:

> The constitutional need for equal protection does not shackle the legislature. It has the widest discretion in classifying those who are to be regulated and taxed. Only if the grouping is without any reasonable basis, and so entirely arbitrary, is it forbidden. Abstract symmetry or mathematical nicety are not requisites. The selection need not depend on scientific or marked differences

[19] *Buck* v. *Bell*, 274 U.S. 200 (1900). See also *McGowan* v. *Maryland*, 366 U.S. 420 (1961).

in things or persons or their relations. If any state of facts reasonably can be conceived that would sustain a classification, the existence of that state of facts as a basis for the passage of the law must be assumed. The burden is on him who assails a classification to show that it does not rest on any reasonable basis.[20]

Three state supreme courts recently confirmed this interpretation and applied it to their state constitutions as well. The plaintiffs in the Vermont land gains tax case contended that under the equal protection clause the legislature acted arbitrarily in stating a purpose (tax relief) that widely diverged from its actual purpose (deterring land speculation), that various classes of landowners and purchasers similarly situated were unequally taxed, and that a reasonable basis did not exist for the six-year, scaled-down tax classification. The court rejected all these contentions. It asserted that the legislature could pursue several purposes at the same time, and that the legislature had legitimately sought deterrence of land speculation. The classifications of transferors had to be sustained, the court said, because they were more than minimally related to the statutory purpose. In restating the requirement for relationship between purpose and classification, the court remarked "[The requirement says] no more than . . . that the relationship between classification and objective cannot be so tenuous as to require a Rube Goldberg structure of causal connections to establish a rational nexus."[21] And finally, regarding the choice of six years as the period during which the tax would be applied to land exchanges, the court summarized what it believed to be the applicable law in terms that heavily favored wide legislative discretion: "a quantitative distinction created by the legislature will be upheld unless it is so 'wide of the mark' that it cannot be said to tend toward achievement of any legislative purpose it might be said to serve."[22]

In the bottle bill case, the Oregon Supreme Court rejected the theory that soft drink manufacturers must be treated on a par with individuals who have been protected against discrimination based on race, religion, sex, and restriction on travel. The court showed that the ban on nonreturnables and the 5-cent deposit on returnables could hardly be called "wholly irrelevant" to achievement of

---

[20] *Allied American Co.* v. *Commissioner*, 219 Md. 607, 623 (1971).
[21] *Andrews* v. *Lathrop*, 315 A.2d at 864.
[22] Ibid.

the state's objectives. It also pointed out that the U.S. Supreme Court had provided an answer to plaintiffs' claim that the bill dealt piecemeal with the state's solid waste and litter problem. "It is no requirement of equal protection that all evils of the same genus be eradicated or none at all."[23] The Supreme Court of Illinois also recently upheld a sanitary district ordinance imposing a surcharge on industrial plant effluents against a claim that the surcharge ordinance was arbitrarily limited only to industries and manufacturers. The court cited additional cases rejecting the all-or-nothing approach, saying: "We cannot regard as unreasonable *per se* a regulation applying only to those whose activities create a substantial burden or load on the facilities of the District."[24] Thus charges plans do not appear to be in any danger from equal protection claims. In particular, those designed to apply to one parameter only of an environmental problem (e.g., bottles, land speculation, biological oxygen demand, sulfur dioxide), or to reach only the worst sources, would very likely survive equal protection challenges under federal and state constitutions.

The equal protection cases indicate how the courts will probably dispose of challenges to the actual level at which a charge is set (e.g., 20 cents per pound of sulfur dioxide) or to the measurement technique adopted in setting the charge (social damage, cost of abatement, industry-wide incentives). Unless the legislature's choices are very wide of any reasonable mark, the absence of mathematical or logical exactness will not suffice to void the charge.

From time to time the courts have toyed with a stronger notion of due process which would require that legislative proposals contain a measure of fairness in their basic contents that goes beyond procedural fairness. Charges proposals conceivably could be examined on this ground for "substantive" due process, but the likelihood is at present quite small. The Supreme Court has not struck down social and economic legislation on substantive due process grounds since the Depression. In a 1968 attempt to invoke the doctrine, the Court dismissed the challenge without discussion.[25] The Oregon Supreme Court in its bottle bill decision gave the argu-

23 *Railway Express Co.* v. *New York,* 336 U.S. 106, 110 (1949).

24 *Chicago Allis* v. *Sanitary District* (Ill. Sup. Ct. 1972) *Environment Reporter Cases* vol. 4, pp. 1642, 1646.

25 *Firemen* v. *Chicago, R.I. and P.R. Co.,* 393 U.S. 129, 143 (1968).

ment hardly any attention at all. Thus, despite the view that the doctrine may be enjoying a modest rebirth, it is unlikely that charges plans will encounter serious difficulty with substantive due process.

The due process clauses of federal and state constitutions also require that the taking of private property for public purposes be surrounded by certain procedural safeguards and that just compensation be paid. In an out-and-out condemnation of land for a public purpose, the government expects to meet a high procedural standard and to pay a just price for the property. Difficulties begin, however, when the private party asserts that a regulatory measure so severely curtails the use of property that a "taking" has occurred despite the legislature's intent merely to regulate. Charges plans could be challenged, although we do not think successfully, through a variation of this familiar argument.

The discussion of legislative power should have made clear that the police and commerce powers are extremely broad and already have had built upon them major environmental regulatory programs that substantially curtail the way private property may be used if the use impairs environmental quality. Even in the case of water pollution, where an argument can be made that a property right exists to the waste transport capacity of streams, the Federal Water Pollution Control Act Amendments of 1972 contemplate elimination of discharges by 1985, without compensation. Property rights to other types of medial pollution are more far fetched, yet even in this hardest case of water pollution, property rights vis-à-vis the public do not seem likely to be sustained.

Charges as "Penalties": Delegation, Criminal Due Process, Trial by Jury

We are inclined to believe that the most serious challenge to charges plans likely to confront the courts rests upon the claim that despite the market theory used to justify them, charges are in fact monetary penalties and therefore must be subjected to the constitutional safeguards provided in the criminal law. If the courts hold that the designation of charges plans as "civil" regulatory schemes is in effect a subterfuge, then the charges approach is in peril. Each charge assessment might conceivably be burdened with such a

panoply of judicial review, jury trials, notice requirements, discovery, and other procedural guarantees that efficient administration would become impossible. In the state courts, plans might be held unconstitutional as an impermissible usurpation of judicial power. Charges plans would literally be "due processed" to death.

We think, however, that the resemblance between charges and penalties is superficial and that criminal safeguards are inappropriate to the charges approach. If courts were to adopt this view, they would have seriously misunderstood the purpose and effect of the charges strategy.

Through application of the due process clauses of the Fifth and Fourteenth amendments, the requirement of trial by jury in the Seventh Amendment, and the separation of powers doctrine of both federal and state constitutions, the courts attempt to provide careful protection for the rights of the criminally accused. Efficiency and speed are properly sacrificed to avoid the risk of improper conviction. As a result, however, criminal cases languish on judicial dockets, defendants settle on terms favorable to them, and prosecutors apply a different logic and morality to improper acts than does the agency charged with remedying a particular social evil. In short, active resistance and delay are on the side of the defendant who is required to pay a "criminal" charge.

Charges do bear a superficial resemblance to the criminal penalties that are levied under regulatory statutes. Both appear initially to be used to modify social conduct that has been disapproved by the legislature. Where regulatory standards have been set and charges are provided as an incentive to meet the standard, "civil" charges seem at first glance to function in the same way as the "criminal" sanctions and money penalties that may also be imposed to attain the same goal.

The similarities between charges and penalties, however, are heavily outweighed by their differences. Charges are not punitively imposed. No determination of guilt or innocence is made, nor is the polluter's character impugned. The behavior for which charges are levied is not "evil in itself," as, for example, are robbery and homicide. In fact, most activities on which charges would be placed provide great social benefits. The conduct "charged" is socially desirable; conduct "penalized" is not.

The charges approach is an entire regulatory strategy complete in itself, of which the money charge is an integral part, whereas criminal money penalties are enforcement devices tacked on to the final phases of regulatory implementation plans to give them teeth. Standing alone, penalties are hardly a strategy at all. The legislature could even use money penalties (e.g., triple charges payments) to achieve adequate enforcement of statutes based on the theory of charges.

The differences run even deeper. Criminal penalties typically are not scaled in small increments, as are charges; rather, criminal penalties usually are pinpointed on infrequent acts that break hard-and-fast rules to which the defendant is expected to conform. Penalties levied for occasional breaches are thus fundamentally unlike charges, which seek to cause changes in economic decision making at the margin and which are assessed incrementally on a course of conduct. Occasionally legislatures and courts justify penalties as costs of control or as restorations of loss to society, but the context usually makes it clear that these bodies are not thinking of economic cost internalizations. The amount of a penalty, moreover, is not predicated on an analysis of the economic behavior of the defendant as much as it is upon the gravity of the offense. Civil tort liability for nuisance damages offers a much closer analogy to charges.

The manner in which charges plans are put into operation further highlights the differences. Charges are part of the ongoing task of regulation and are chosen to achieve optional abatement levels within an environmentally motivated plan. Under the agency plan, charges are prospectively set for all polluters in a class and when functioning properly are automatically and uniformly administered thereafter, whereas penalties ordinarily are levied after the fact on a case-by-case basis, with a good deal of agency discretion about how much, whom, and when to fine. In the case of penalties, crackdowns to make an "example" of a defendant may take place, a possibility that does not exist under charges plans.

In view of these contrasts, courts will probably accept the charges approach on its merits as a new and unique regulatory strategy. Legislatures can play an important role in ensuring this

result by stating clearly that charges revenues are an incidental by-product of the regulatory strategy and are not intended to be criminal sanctions.

It follows that the legislature should be able to enact a streamlined administrative procedure, containing a minimum of red tape in its enforcement and review provisions, with no more constitutional difficulty than it has encountered in enacting conventional regulatory statutes. Established judicial doctrines that limit arbitrary abuse and unlawful extensions of power by agencies and the constitutional guarantee against arbitrary legislative exercise of power both provide the courts with sufficient authority to invalidate charges schemes that clearly are confiscatory or are unnecessarily drastic. In the instance of charges plans, a higher doctrinal standard would serve no useful social purpose.

However, should the legislatures and courts nevertheless insist on viewing charges as penal in nature, all is not lost. "Civil" monetary penalties are included in the enforcement provisions of many statutes. While civil monetary penalties may carry with them a slightly higher standard of procedural due process than might be administratively convenient, the charges approach could probably still be implemented. Some feel that a civil monetary penalty may offer a more appropriate way to categorize the environmental charge, which may seem to some to fall somewhere between civil and criminal extremes. The Administrative Conference of the United States has recommended wider use of civil monetary penalties as an administratively imposed enforcement device in the environmental area.[26] This approach may save the charges concept from superfluous constraints under the criminal law if a legislature or the courts want to impose a higher standard of accountability on the government because a monetary exaction is involved.

What are the due process standards surrounding civil monetary penalties? They have never been precisely stated. Although existing standards are higher than we think necessary to safeguard industrial polluters' rights in a charges system, the content of such standards appears to be evolving toward greater administrative flexibility. Certainly they have been in greater use in recent years.[27]

[26] Administrative Conference of the United States, Recommendation 72-6: Civil Money Penalties as a Sanction (adopted December 14, 1972).

[27] Harvey Goldschmid, "An Evaluation of the Present and Potential Use of Civil

The Administrative Conference, which plainly was thinking of traditional criminal penalties and fines rather than economic charges, endorsed the expanded use of civil monetary penalties on the grounds that they provide a speedy, flexible enforcement mechanism, that they measure culpability more precisely, that they avoid harsh all-or-nothing decisions (e.g., on license revocations), and that they avoid the stigma of criminal convictions. The standards for assessing such a penalty, however, still would remain high in the Conference's view. Penalties would be assessed by the agencies, but if the agency or polluter requested it, the assessment would have to take place on the record in a quasi-judicial hearing, which in a charges plan would require advance notice of the intent to levy the charge, an opportunity to challenge the levy before imposition of the charge, provision for a hearing with counsel, and other safeguards. While jury trials and complete redeterminations of the charge by a court would be precluded (they are available in criminal cases), an appeal could be taken to a federal court of appeals, which could at least satisfy itself that the charge was supported by substantial evidence in the record compiled at the agency hearing.

Overzealous adoption of these safeguards could block simple enforcement of the charges approach. But legislatures and agencies could do much to ensure efficient decisions by writing legislation and implementing guidelines to eliminate unnecessary delay and challenge. Furthermore, as mentioned, the courts have yet to determine the minimum content of procedural due process for civil money penalties. The leading Supreme Court case on the subject held that a $360,000 penalty under the Internal Revenue Code was civil in nature, relying on Congress's intent to make it civil, the historic use of civil tax penalties, the legitimate regulatory and revenue purposes involved, the reimbursement for costs of regulation and for loss, and the relative freedom of the sanction from criminal overtones.[28] Environmental charges easily meet the standards of the Internal Revenue Service procedures, and on their merits could justify a considerably more streamlined procedure

---

Money Penalties as a Sanction by Federal Administrative Agencies, A Report Prepared for the Committee on Compliance and Enforcement of the Administrative Conference of the United States" (November 17, 1972), p. 9 *ff.*

[28] *Helvering* v. *Mitchell,* 303 U.S. 391 (1938).

under the Supreme Court's test. Agencies already possess far greater administrative power through their powers to deny and suspend licenses than charges plans would confer.

The procedural standards that charges plans must meet are one thing, the constitutionality of executive imposition of money penalties is another. The question is insignificant in federal law, but in state law it poses an important difficulty. The Supreme Court has never held that the federal judicial power was improperly vested in a federal administrative agency. In the *Sushine Coal* case,[29] decided in 1940, the Supreme Court stated that to have held that there was an invalid delegation of judicial power would have turned "back the clock on at least a half century of administrative law." Many state courts, however, are still writing opinions on nondelegation of which the best benches of the nineteenth century would be proud. State charges plans, where characterized as money penalty plans, are jeopardized by those decisions.[30]

Burdens on Interstate Commerce and Preemption:
State Concerns

State charges legislation will be invalidated if it impedes the "flow of commerce" in national markets, or if it and preexisting federal legislation pursue mutually exclusive solutions to the same environmental problem. The federal power to regulate commerce has already been discussed, but it was only mentioned that the power includes the obligation to protect the national economy against parochial state action.[31] Here the federal safeguards are examined in more detail.

We will also consider whether Congress's recent attacks on environmental problems have so blanketed the field with comprehensive federal solutions that no place is left for state efforts. To anticipate, we conclude that the key federal statutes expressly provide that state law is not preempted and that most environmental problems are still open to state regulation so long as the legislation complements preexisting federal plans.

[29] *Sunshine Coal* v. *Adkins*, 310 U.S. 381 (1940).
[30] But see *Waukegan* v. *Pollution Control Board*, 311 N.E. 2d 146 (Ill. Sup. Ct. 1974).
[31] See p. 110.

COMMERCE CLAUSE RESTRAINTS ON STATE LEGISLATION. The purpose of the commerce clause remains what it was in the beginning: to assure that commercial enterprises in all states have substantially equal access to national markets. But the guarantee of the commerce clause does not mean that the state legislatures are forbidden to enact legislation that unfavorably affects out-of-state businesses. The courts have attempted to strike a balance between the exercise of state power and the protection of interstate commerce. Under this balancing of interests, the courts have traded off protection of the status quo in interstate commerce against the harm that would be caused if the local problem went unregulated. Charges, too, must be subject to this balancing and are likely to be scrutinized closely, because they are expressly premised upon economic intervention.

The Supreme Court recently stated the general test for the validity of state statutes affecting interstate commerce:

> Where the statute regulates evenhandedly to effectuate a legitimate local public interest, and its effects on interstate commerce are only incidental, it will be upheld unless the burden imposed on such commerce is clearly excessive in relation to the putative local benefits.[32]

The Oregon Supreme Court's rejection of a challenge to the state's bottle bill, for example, rested ultimately upon the balancing of interests approach. The Oregon court found that the bottle bill did not confer a competitive advantage upon Oregon's industry and refused to upset the legislative judgment that balanced the economic loss restricted to certain elements of the beverage industry against the broader loss to the general public which enactment of the bottle bill would avoid. The land and revenues tied up in solid waste disposal, the cost of litter collection on highways and in Oregon's public parks, the depletion of mineral and energy resources, the injuries to humans and animals caused by discarded pull tops, and the aesthetic blight on the landscape were all thought to be burdens borne by Oregon's public that merited a limited inroad on interstate commerce.[33] Since the state had adopted a reasonable means of achieving its goal, the statutory scheme could not be overturned.

[32] *Pike* v. *Bruce Church, Inc.*, 397 U.S. 137, 142 (1970).
[33] *American Can Co.* v. *Oregon Liquor Control Commission*, 517 P.2d at 702–703.

The Oregon court saw additional merit in the particular scheme adopted. It stated that the freedom of state legislatures to choose any reasonable means to achieve their purposes ensures that each state is "a laboratory for innovation and experimentation in a healthy federal system." Charges plans need such laboratories of experimentation and benefit from this judicial attitude. "The bottle bill is now unique; it may later be regarded as seminal."[34]

The courts have developed a few special rules that channel particular applications of the general balancing approach. These rules may affect charges proposals in particular ways. If a method of regulation is available, for example, which would cause a lesser impact on interstate commerce, the particular measure may be voided. In the context of charges plans, this rule may mean that a close comparison of the relative effects of conventional regulatory strategies and the charges approach will have to be made.

Further, states cannot screen measures favoring in-state industry behind suspect exercises of the police power. Such legislation has been held invalid in a long series of cases in which the legislature's motives appeared to be less than simon-pure. Had Oregon been the only state with a thriving recyclable beverage container industry, and few pull-top nonreturnable cans were produced and used there, its ban-and-deposit law might have been in serious trouble. As it happened, the law fell equally upon in-state and out-of-state enterprises.

To ensure the "free flow" of commerce, the courts have had to focus on excessive state regulation of the means of transport. Rail, air, water, and highway travel are all suitable candidates for application of the charges approach. Charges have been proposed for vehicle weight, fuel spill, and decibel levels, to take the most prominent examples.

Interstate transportation is especially vulnerable to inconsistent state regulation, as shown by a long series of cases about such variabilia as train length and crew sizes, truck mud flaps, and vessel smoke emissions. This constraint on state action is not important to the charges approach, however, because charges fortunately are fungible; they could apply to a form of transportation without different states imposing inconsistent requirements for equipment, personnel, and the like. There would be no burden on commerce

[34] Ibid., p. 700.

from variations in state charge rates. Further, one purpose of charges may be to return to the public a rough monetary equivalent of its losses for the use of its common property resources. Different charges among states could be justified as the result of different states' estimates of the social damage caused.

The courts used to phrase the test for conflicting state legislation in terms of the basic nature of the subject matter regulated. If the subject matter of the state legislation is national in its nature, the cases held, so that it admits of only one uniform system of regulation, then the area requires exclusive legislation by Congress.[35] The "need-for-national-uniformity" standard is a corollary of the "substantial-interference-with-commerce" standard discussed above. The excesses of a state statute which causes severe out-of-state impacts might be remedied if that statute were enacted nationwide.

The uniform national application test is, we think, relatively neutral as it applies to charges plans. Environmental quality can be fairly said to be of both local and national concern, with emphasis, if any is expected, on local concern, and can be regulated on both levels. Most charges plans can function effectively without unreasonable impacts on interstate commerce, but they also could be applied nationwide with relative ease. The choice then comes down to a political one about how the nation would like to allocate regulation among federal and state governments and about the strategies for control which each would prefer to employ, all of which carries the discussion to Congress's decisions about the level of government which will control, and thus to the issue of federal preemption.

PREEMPTION. We have just seen that the courts may find that an environmental problem which a state would like to control requires a uniform nationwide system of regulation, even if Congress has not yet acted to provide that system. In the environmental area, however, Congress usually has already taken some type of action, and the issue shifts to whether congressional preemption prevents the state from enacting its own plan.

In cases where state law overlaps with federal authority, the supremacy of federal law requires that the state law yield to the federal authority. Congress, however, may permit the states to reg-

[35] *Cooley* v. *Board of Wardens*, 53 U.S. (12 How.) 299 (1851).

ulate in the area. Where Congress speaks plainly, the question is easily settled: if Congress acted lawfully in allowing the state to legislate, or if it expressly preempted the field, there is little more to be said. More often than not, though, Congress is silent on the state role. In such cases the courts must do the best they can to infer Congress's intent from the existing statutory language. In reading the statutes, the courts sometimes inject their own view about the best allocation of authority among the federal and the state governments.

Mere overlap of power, or even of functioning regulatory schemes, has not been enough under our pragmatic federalism to cause the Congress or the courts to vest regulatory authority automatically in one level of government alone. The Congress has sometimes permitted the overlap of regulatory programs, sometimes encouraged state solutions, and sometimes preempted specific problems for exclusive federal control. The courts also look at the particular circumstances. The Supreme Court in the same year (1973) held that state regulation of radiation from nuclear plants and of the noise from jets had been preempted, but that the regulation of oil spills from ships had not.[36] Charges plans are likely to be afforded the same mixed reception, depending upon the unique circumstances of the problem under consideration.

In the environmental area, Congress has stated the general view that the "primary responsibility" for implementing the national environmental policy, as developed in a welter of federal statutes and particularly in the National Environmental Policy Act, rests with state and local governments.[37] Federal air and water quality and solid waste control laws contain similar declarations. In reviewing claims of federal preemption, courts have stated their awareness of these provisions. Furthermore, environmental regulation has traditionally been a police power function. Only in recent years has the federal government moved heavily into the area. Hence, state charges proposals would at least start out with a broad policy favoring their validity. The specifics of any particular problem, however, may overcome this presumption.

The law of preemption, then, is highly specific. We must examine key statutes to see if Congress or the courts have provided

36 Soper, "Constitutional Framework," p. 83.
37 Environmental Quality Improvement Act of 1970, 42 U.S.C. §4372 (b)(2).

an answer, or even clues, as to whether existing federal legislation would preempt state charges proposals in particular areas. Federal statutes protecting water and air quality are of course especially important.

The Clean Air Act of 1970 provides that the states may adopt "standards" and "requirements" that result in higher quality than that required by the federal standards, but the state may not lower a standard.[38] It appears that the Clean Air Act carefully preserved the view expressed ten years earlier by the Supreme Court in the *Huron Cement* case:

> Legislation designed to free from pollution the very air that people breathe clearly falls within the exercise of even the most traditional concept of what is compendiously known as the police power. In the exercise of that power, the states and their instrumentalities may act, in many areas of interstate commerce and maritime activities, concurrently with the federal government.[39]

The language chosen by Congress leaves us with some lingering doubt that Congress intended to do more than authorize states to set higher standards than those which the state would have had to impose for the minimal satisfaction of the federal scheme. Congress did not prohibit the creation of a separate regulatory mechanism, such as a supplementary charges plan, but neither did it appear to contemplate more than the possibility of stricter state applications of the standards and procedures within the framework specified in detail in the federal legislation. Again, as so often in questions regarding preemption, the courts would have to infer the congressional intent.

The Clean Air Act provides several specific exceptions to the general rule favoring higher state standards. State regulation of certain specific forms of air pollution was rather plainly preempted by the Act. The Act places exclusive authority to set emission standards for new motor vehicles in the federal government.[40] Preemption, however, does not extend to older vehicles, and litigation has confirmed that the states are free to require older models to meet high state emissions standards.[41] The Act also

38 42 U.S.C. §1857d-1 (1970).

39 *Huron Cement Co.* v. *Detroit*, 362 U.S., 442.

40 42 U.S.C. §1857f-1 (1970).

41 Thomas Jorling, "Air Pollution Control," in Dolgin and Guilbert, *Federal Environmental Law*, pp. 1128–30.

expressly preserved state authority to restrict the use or movement of motor vehicles.

State regulation of aircraft emissions is also preempted by the Act. The Act preempts state regulation of combustion fuels, but in some limited cases the state may also act.[42] State regulation of radioactive emissions apparently is preempted under the Atomic Energy Act, although thermal air pollution from a nuclear plant would not, under the Atomic Energy Act itself, appear to be preempted.[43]

The Federal Water Pollution Control Act Amendments of 1972 contain a provision which expressly reserves to the states the power to enact water quality controls that set standards stricter than those which the federal act contemplates.[44] As in the Clean Air Act, a state may enact an effluent charge plan so long as it does not excuse the dischargers subject to it from meeting limitations applied under the federal legislation. State effluent charges statutes are not preempted and may be used to achieve a higher level of water quality sooner than the federal act would have required.

Since the goal of the federal act is to press abatement technology to its limits and to end all discharges by 1985, it may be asked if the power of the state to set stricter standards through an effluent charges plan means very much, and if in a decade it will mean anything at all. To answer this question it is worth looking at what the actual requirements of the federal law mean in practice. A closer look shows that there may indeed be room for states to enact charges plans that will be stricter in *actual* operation than the federal plan will be in many years.

Under the federal Act, state effluent charges laws cannot allow a discharger to release effluents in excess of those specified under the Act's effluent standards, or to reduce water quality below that required by water quality standards, whichever is stricter.

Water quality standards are holdovers from preexisting federal water pollution control law and are based on environmental effects only. As discussed in chapter 4, water quality standards consist of a set of rules defining a required quality for the ambient water. These standards are based on technical information as to the

42 Ibid., p. 1130.
43 Ibid., p. 1125.
44 33 U.S.C. 1370 (1972). See also 33 U.S.C. 1341 (1970).

minimum requirements necessary to sustain various uses of water, such as recreation in or on the water, propagation of fish, and public water supply. In infrequent instances, enforcement of these standards will require that for a given stream, effluents must be *below* levels achievable by technology.

The new federal Act, however, adopts the policy that any pollution is at least to some extent undesirable and sets the goal of reducing it to the maximum extent possible within the limits of our technology. Thus the Act creates stricter technology-based effluent standards which limit dischargers to specific amounts of pollutants that may be discharged. Existing dischargers (other than publicly owned treatment works) are required to adopt the "best practicable control technology currently available" by July 1, 1977, and the "best available technology economically achievable" by July 1, 1983. Publicly owned treatment works must meet similar standards, and new sources must meet standards based on the "best available control technology, processes, operating methods, or other alternatives."

Unless these effluent standards are met, polluters cannot retain the permit which is legally necessary under the Act before making any discharge at all. The difficulty is that the permits, which are currently being issued, can only specify pollution levels to be attained at rather distant future dates. When those dates arrive, permittees undoubtedly will defend themselves against revocation by resorting to technological arguments under the technology-based phrasing of the Act.

In these disputes it will finally become clear that the 1977 and 1983 standards require some form of trading off of marginal costs of abatement against marginal improvements in water quality. That this can only be the result is clear from the Act, which states specifically that in setting the 1977 standards there must be "consideration of the total cost of application of technology in relation to the effluent reduction benefits to be achieved from such application,"[45] and in setting 1983 standards there must be taken "into account . . . the cost of achieving such effluent reduction."[46] The lack of any greater specificity regarding how the 1983 standards are to be set results very plainly from the inability of the House and

[45] 33 U.S.C. 1314(b)(1)(B) (1972).
[46] 33 U.S.C. 1314(b)(2)(B) (1972).

Senate conferees to come anywhere near agreement. For the 1983 and new source standards, perhaps the only fair inference from the legislative history is that cost should simply be considered as another factor in the overall determination of whether a particular technology is "available."[47]

The achievement, then, of the lofty goals (1977, 1983, 1985) of the federal Act is predicated upon technological achievement and its full implementation, a process the Environmental Protection Agency must police. This asks a great deal of a regulatory agency. Under the 1972 Amendments, EPA must plunge deeply into the scientific and engineering aspects of water pollution control. As able as the agency and its scientifically trained personnel are, they cannot become the equals of their counterparts in industry, who have the further advantage of access to corporate performance records and other proprietary data. When legal challenges are mounted because a permit has been revoked in late 1977 or late 1983, the burden will rest heavily upon EPA to prove that its permittees have not met the statutory standard.

If the technology-based standards of the federal Act prove inadequate to secure swimmable water by 1983 and no discharge by 1985, it is not at all clear that EPA can close plants down or even reduce their productivity in order to achieve the 1983 or 1985 goals. By its reference to "economic or social dislocations in the affected community," the Act appears only to envisage the closing of existing plants, or possibly a ban on future plant construction, or another "alternative control strategy."[48] In view of the cost–benefit balancing discussed above, one may at least doubt whether the Act's tougher passages (notably §302) will ever be used to impose such drastic remedies.

If economic and technical factors may be lawfully invoked under the 1972 Amendments to forestall for an indefinite period the achievement of the 1983 and 1985 goals, then state effluent charges plans appear in a more favorable light. The total scheme of federal–state control under the Act appears to be in much greater need of supplementary assistance than first thought. First, to dispose of the legal objection with which we began the discussion, the

[47] Robert Zener, "Water Pollution Control," in Dolgin and Guilbert, *Federal Environmental Law,* p. 699.
[48] Ibid., pp. 725–26.

flat federal ban on water pollution may not, for much longer than the decade to come, preempt possible state effluent charges plans that assume that at least some chargeable pollution will continue to occur. Second, effluent charges would be exceptionally well timed if they were imposed at the moment when managers were trying to convince pollution control officials that they had improperly gathered and incorrectly interpreted technological and economic data on polluting industries and firms. The steady additional economic disincentive provided by charges plans would hasten management decision making toward meeting the federal Act's goals. The way for polluters to avoid sizable economic consequences in the present would be to develop and implement less polluting production techniques and abatement technologies.

The Setting of Charges Levels by Administrative Agencies: The Delegation Doctrine

A few pages earlier we discussed what would happen if charges were viewed as criminal penalties which administrative agencies set and collected. There we discussed the view that criminal fines can be levied only by courts because the constitutional requirement that legislative, judicial, and executive powers be separately exercised entails imposition of criminal sanctions by the judicial branch only. The separation of powers doctrine has another side which is taken up very briefly here. The challenge can be made that delegation to the executive branch of the essentially legislative function of determining tax rates is impermissible under the separation of powers doctrine. A charge, if viewed as a tax, could therefore be set only by the legislature, which is empowered to *lay* and collect taxes. The administering agency would consequently be deprived of flexibility in setting charges by formal rule-making procedures.

The last time the Supreme Court voided federal legislation on the grounds that it impermissibly delegated a legislative function to an administrative agency was in 1936. If Congress wants an administrative agency to set the levels of charges, the federal courts are not likely to hold that the Congress itself is required to perform that function. If Congress spells out the criteria for setting the charge, indicating the classes of polluters, conditions, and

pollutants to be reached, and defines the procedural requirements which the agency must meet in reaching a decision, a challenge based on the separation of powers doctrine is not likely to be given serious consideration. As pointed out, variable monetary penalties already are levied by the federal agencies, and the Administrative Conference of the United States has recommended wider use of them.

State courts have applied the separation of powers doctrine much more stringently and continue to void legislative acts as impermissible delegations of legislative authority. Many of these cases involve delegation to local low-level officialdom, however, not to state agencies such as those which carry out statewide environmental control programs. Even delegations to local authorities allowing them to impose user fees and sewer surcharges typically survive challenge, if a challenge is mounted at all.[49]

We can think of no reason why the presence of a revenue-generating component in a regulatory proposal should prompt the courts to behave any differently from the way they already have in upholding vague statutory delegations. Agencies already rely on broad statutory mandates in imposing permit and licensing requirements that effectively cost as much or more than charges schemes contemplate. The denial of agency permissions, predicated upon regulations which Congress could have had no idea would be promulgated, have even "cost" companies the ultimate price by regulating them out of existence.

Monitoring, Inspection, and the Protection of Trade Secrets

Monitoring

Most charges plans would have to depend upon an accurate report of chargeable emissions compiled by the persons in charge of the source of emissions itself. The administrative difficulty which an agency would face if it actually operated the monitoring system

---

[49] See, e.g., the Chicago Allis case. Regarding the possibility that nondelegation principles may be more strictly applied to administrative determination of charges, see *National Cable Television* v. *United States*, 415 U.S. 336 (1974).

would be overwhelming in most charges proposals. The preferable alternative is to require sources to report their emissions, with the agency policing the system by specifying the components of the system and by spot-checking its operation through site inspections and examinations of record books.

The agency administering the charges plan may have to specify in detail the particular monitoring devices and record-keeping techniques to be employed. The agency may want to promulgate performance criteria for the recording instruments, certify certain instruments as adequate for use in the charges plan, and specify the conditions and times for which periodic sampling rather than continuous monitoring is appropriate. The agency may want to provide its own inspectors to visit premises where the basic data is gathered in order to check instrument reliability and record-keeping systems. Unannounced inspections would help ensure accuracy, and the agency could promulgate rules for such inspections. (These requirements may be obviated where charges are estimated from production-related parameters, with the firm having the opportunity to show that its effluents are lower than the estimates.)

A challenge based on the mere existence of a complex record-keeping requirement is unlikely to be sustained. Similar monitoring systems have already been widely accepted in control programs as a necessary adjunct of modern regulatory strategies. A reporting requirement could conceivably be so onerous as to constitute a taking of property without compensation, but the burden imposed would have to be very great indeed.

A 1972 case decided by the Illinois Supreme Court[50] gives some indication of the permissible burden of monitoring costs that may be imposed on a polluter to ensure the proper functioning of a water quality control program. Under a state enabling statute, the Metropolitan Sanitary District of Greater Chicago imposed a surcharge on industrial waste discharges in excess of 3.6 million gallons annually. The amount of the charge depended upon the volume, BOD, and suspended solids content of the wastewater discharges. The individual plants were made responsible for measuring the amount and content of the wastewater subject to the charge. Each plant was required by regulation to provide each

[50] Ibid.

of its waste outlets with a manhole or sampling chamber containing specified sampling equipment. In the litigation, the plaintiffs maintained that the 2,000 companies subject to the ordinance would have to pay as much as $200 million for the equipment and time lost installing it.

The plaintiffs first maintained that the sampling chamber and metering device requirements were so onerous that they constituted a taking of property without due process. The court quickly disposed of this argument, simply citing the traditional reliance on the police power to create waste disposal systems. Next the plaintiffs argued that less onerous measurement techniques were available and that it was a denial of due process for the District to impose costly ones through its ordinance. The court examined the plaintiffs' evidence, but could not find that the system was unreasonable, or that plaintiffs had actually shown unduly oppressive costs. Nor could the court lend credence to plaintiffs' claim that they had been denied the equal protection of law because the ordinance applied to industrial and manufacturing processes alone. As mentioned above, the legislature is not obligated by the equal protection requirement to regulate all or none of the sources of a social problem.

SELF-INCRIMINATION.   While heavy reporting requirements may not in themselves be unlawful, the safeguards of the criminal law may again come into play if the legislature imposes charges as criminal monetary penalties. If the courts insist that these are punitive assessments despite attempts to categorize them as non-punitive, or if information reported under a charges plan can be used for criminal prosecutions under other statutes, the Fifth Amendment safeguards against self-incrimination may apply. Mandatory monitoring and surrender of data would then supply the agency with information for criminal prosecutions, possibly in contravention of the privilege against self-incriminatory actions.

The privilege against self-incrimination, while it cannot be dismissed as a misplaced attempt to protect privacy, would probably not be sympathetically received by the courts if it were invoked against a requirement for self-monitoring. First, a corporation may not claim the privilege on its own behalf. Nor can an employee

refuse to make corporate records available on the grounds that the corporation or another employee might be incriminated.

Second, reporting requirements basically serve a nonpunitive regulatory purpose, even if occasionally a report may contain information that could be used in a criminal prosecution. The Supreme Court has distinguished reporting requirements that are neutral on their face and directed to the public at large from requirements that are directed at a small group inherently suspect of criminal activity.[51] In other words, the Court has not automatically given complete protection to persons required to report just because there is some hazard of prosecution. Rather, the reasonable need for noncriminal regulatory reporting schemes has been balanced against constitutional safeguards of fairness, protection of personal privacy, and avoidance of torture and brutality.

We have already had occasion to consider how charges and criminal monetary penalties differ. The same kind of considerations apply here in distinguishing an incriminatory reporting requirement from an innocuous regulatory one. The privilege protects individuals from criminal prosecution; charges apply to corporate behavior. The companies subject to charges are not inherently suspected of criminal activity. Reporting requirements applied to them are neutral in effect and are intended to be part of a nonpunitive regulatory system. The area involves only a few criminal statutes directed to individuals, and the hazard of prosecution of either corporations or individuals has been very remote.

A difficulty arises where information required for assessing charges could be used against the supplier in a coexisting system of standards enforceable by criminal process. Assuming that individuals, as opposed to corporations themselves, can be made personally liable under the standards system, the charges statute should perhaps include an immunity from prosecution for individuals who supply incriminating information in order to comply with the charges plan.

In theory, individuals could abuse this proposed immunity by rushing to reveal chargeable emissions under the charges plan in order to obtain immunity from prosecution under the harsher

[51] *Albertson* v. *Subversive Activities Control Board,* 382 U.S. 70 (1965); *Marchetti* v. *United States,* 390 U.S. 39 (1968).

criminal sanctions that back up the regulatory standards. The charges system would benefit from the flow of full and accurate information, but "lawbreakers" would escape the punishment intended for them for exceeding the regulatory standard. Yet the injustice is less of a threat than it seems. Once information is divulged, the supplier's practices are better known for the next time, whether under the charges plan or the criminally sanctioned standard. Bad publicity would follow "taking the Fifth," even if the request for immunity were legally successful. The supplier would acquire a particularly bad reputation at the agency charged with environmental protection, where investigatory action might follow to prevent a similar occurrence in the future. For such individuals, the self-reporting scheme could clearly be policed in a more adversarial fashion.

SURPRISE INSPECTIONS.   Inspection procedures for charges plans would have to satisfy the protection provided by the Fourth Amendment against unreasonable search and seizure, especially if a criminal sanction is to be available for violations of the reporting requirements. Until recently, an administrative search of commercial premises required a search warrant.[52] Issuance of the warrant took a lot of time and a special showing that a warrant was justified under the circumstances. Routine, "nonsuspicious" checks were effectively precluded.

In 1972, however, the Supreme Court held that a warrant was not necessary for search of a gun seller's stockroom, if conducted under the search provisions of the Gun Control Act of 1968. Parts of the Court's reasoning could apply directly to surprise and routine searches under charges plans:

> If the law is to be properly enforced and inspection made effective, inspections without warrant must be deemed reasonable official conduct under the Fourth Amendment. If inspection is to be effective and serve as a credible deterrent, unannounced, even frequent, inspections are essential. In this context, the prerequisite of a warrant could easily frustrate inspection; and if the necessary flexibility as to time, scope, and frequency is to be preserved, the protections afforded by a warrant would be negligible.

52 Comment, "The Effluent Fee Approach for Controlling Air Pollution," *Duke Law Journal* (1970) pp. 943, 973.

It is also plain that inspections for compliance with the Gun Control Act pose only limited threats to the dealer's justifiable expectations of privacy. When a dealer chooses to engage in this pervasively regulated business and to accept a federal license, he does so with the knowledge that his business records, firearms, and ammunition will be subject to effective inspection. . . .

We have little difficulty in concluding that where, as here, regulatory inspections further an urgent federal interest and the possibilities of abuse and the threat to privacy are not of impressive dimensions, the inspection may proceed without a warrant where specifically authorized by statute.[53]

In order to place the financial and administrative burden of monitoring upon the parties paying the charge, who, not coincidentally, are well placed to measure total emissions accurately, the legislature will need to rely upon surprise plant inspections. As with the gun control law, surprise is crucial. Moreover, the risk of abuse of individual liberties is slight, since charges plans will apply primarily to businesses. Criminal safeguards are inappropriate in any event, because charges plans are nonpunitive in nature. Surprise inspections would not be used to obtain criminal convictions or to unearth criminal evidence; rather, they would be used to ensure the integrity of regulatory environmental control programs.

Conclusion

Charges plans form a new category of regulatory legislation. As such, they share characteristics with other regulatory techniques, but in the final analysis they stand on their own unique footing. This is as true from the perspective of the law as it is from the economic, political, and engineering perspectives. However, the concept, which is still in its infancy, has not been fully tested in the courts. When it is, we expect that the courts will accept it as a new and unique legislative strategy, rather than seeking to understand charges as conventional legislative devices such as taxes, penalties, or fees.

[53] *United States* v. *Biswell,* 406 U.S. 311, 316 (1972).

Many different sources of governmental power could be invoked to legitimatize the legislature's imposition of charges plans, although we think the commerce and police power are the most logical choices, because charges perform a regulatory function. In constitutional law, one leg to stand on is as good as two. Any single valid constitutional power—commerce, police, tax—is sufficient underpinning for the exercise of legislative authority. However, if the legislature relies solely on the tax power, or if it imposes the charge as a penalty predicated on a theory of punishment, the charge might conceivably be vulnerable. The courts would try to ascertain the primary purpose of the legislation. Is it regulation? Is it punishment? Is it revenue? At best, the economic theory that supports the charges concept would be understood and accepted by the courts so that the regulatory nature of the approach prevailed. At worst, the courts might scuttle part or all of the plan as an illegal application of the tax and regulatory powers, relying on the arguments discussed, and we hope refuted, in this chapter.

The legislature can play an important role in ensuring that plans which it enacts do not run afoul of the courts. While the legislature cannot by a simple expression of desire make an unconstitutional act constitutional or an illegal action legal, the courts try very hard to view legislation from the legislature's perspective. If the legislature says it is regulating, the courts are not likely to say that it is taxing or punishing. These latter effects will not govern the courts' disposition of a charges plan that is under attack.

6

The Politics of Charges

Introduction

Many of the political problems of charges arise out of a national preference for regulation as the only appropriate legislative means of answering a social need. In a society that values law and relies heavily on it as a means of social control, the effectiveness of outright prohibition of a socially injurious activity, enforced by judicially imposed sanctions, is simply assumed. Prohibition is a response familiar to the general public, and is the instrument of social control most familiar to the legislatures. If direct regulation does not produce the expected results, the assumption is either that the penalties are too weak, the administrators are ineffectual, the existing procedures need to be streamlined, or—an old standby argument—information bases are inadequate.[1]

Hence, passing a "stronger" law can be substituted—over the recurring short run—for an attempt to solve environmental problems. There is no need to think more systematically and to expend political resources trying to build a coalition in favor of a new approach. For this reason much of the debate over environmental legislation turns on whether it is sufficiently "tough," as if the "fault" always lay with willfully antagonistic polluters, and was not ingrained in our social fabric and economic institutions. By

[1] For an insightful discussion of the lure of direct regulation and how existing legal institutions have reacted to the special problems of pollution control, see James E. Krier, "The Pollution Problem and Legal Institutions: A Conceptual Overview," *U.C.L.A. Law Review* vol. 18 (1971) pp. 429–477.

making a regulatory agency responsible for enforcing the law and thrashing out bargains, legislators can gain credit for having passed a tough (and therefore good) law and at the same time temporarily obscure their inability to correct the serious institutional inadequacies which underlie the problem. A strategy such as direct regulation, which involves complicated administrative procedures the impact of which cannot reasonably be expected to be felt for years, is ideally suited to the gratification of this political urge. The choice of a strategy such as a charge system, which resembles an administrative automaton and begins to be felt immediately by those affected, would make it harder to gain both political credit and political accommodations.

Because charges have not been tried on a large scale in the United States, the task of predicting the political environment in which such a system may be initiated and operated is not easy. Political actors whose views would be important in any decision on a charge policy have not been confronted with a charge proposal, have not had to inform themselves about its merits, and therefore provide only weak clues about how they might react to a seriously proposed charge plan. The only real evidence at hand is the positions taken by various groups in the Nixon administration debates over the sulfur oxides tax, some sparse congressional testimony on the Proxmire effluent charge plan for river basins, and the informal reactions of some interested groups to the general concept of charges (see pp. 153–157). Beyond this, positions must be inferred from the general interests that affected groups seem to have.[2]

This chapter deals with four types of political issues. The first involves the special problems that charges face in getting on the public agenda as a serious policy option. The second concerns "interest group politics," the arguments of those powerful groups most affected by a charge system. The third type involves institutional design issues that have important political ramifications. Finally, the fourth deals with the politics of an ongoing charge system— what the political assets and liabilities of a charge system are likely to be in actual operation. This is a question as vital to a sound evaluation of environmental charges as a tally of the economic, administrative, and legal pros and cons.

[2] For a discussion of the problems of political feasibility analysis, see Arnold J. Meltsner, "Political Feasibility and Policy Analysis," *Public Administration Review* vol. 32 (November–December 1972) pp. 859–867.

Getting on the Agenda

Most economists who have studied the issue feel that the charge approach to environmental management is in general superior to the present policy of direct regulation. Yet, strangely enough, there are still very few operating charge programs, and charges have so far received only a cool reception in the Congress. What is the explanation for this disjunction between economists and politicians? Are politicians averse to new policies, unwilling to adopt effective environmental control policies, or merely misinformed? Or do charges present policymakers with more difficult political problems than the present regulatory approach, problems that the economists have ignored?

In this section we try to explain this apparent paradox in order to understand the special difficulties environmental charges have faced—and still face—in getting on the political agenda.

It was only in the 1970s that pollution control policies became a serious political issue. While the 1960s witnessed an increasingly serious intent on the part of Congress to rectify state inaction in the air and water pollution fields, it was only in 1970 in air, and 1972 in water, that Congress acted to revamp clearly inadequate policies. Two implicàtions follow from this historical point. First, opportunities for major policy revision come only infrequently, not annually. It takes a number of years for an existing policy to prove itself ineffective, and there are many other issues competing for a place on the crowded federal agenda, so that chance, as well as political influence, determines when an issue is ripe for reevaluation. The second point is that in 1970 and 1972 the Senate Public Works subcommittee headed by Senator Edmund Muskie did not believe that direct regulation had really been given a fair trial in controlling air and water pollution. In this conclusion they were correct, for the legislation of the 1950s and 1960s reflects the political weakness of its environmental proponents and was so unenforceable that it is almost a misuse of words to call it "regulation."[3] In recent years, scholars have scrutinized the effectiveness of regulatory agencies in many different policy areas. They have concluded that direct regulation fails not only in controlling pollution; it seems to fail generally wherever objectives cannot be easily

[3] See Allen V. Kneese and Charles L. Schultze, *Pollution, Prices, and Public Policy* (Washington, Brookings Institution, 1975).

measured and unambiguously evaluated, and where the political forces favoring regulation become inattentive to the daily decisions of regulatory agencies.[4]

Why do policymakers in the environmental field still think direct regulation is workable? One reason is because sometimes direct regulation is in fact workable, and at other times it is, relatively speaking, the most workable policy in a situation where nothing works very well. Unfortunately, in other situations it is ineffective and inefficient, both absolutely in terms of reaching stated goals, and relative to other conceivable policies. The difficulty is that there is no clear and widely circulated theory that tells public officials the conditions under which the direct enforcement of standards will work, and the conditions under which other strategies are called for.

As pointed out in chapter 1, direct regulation is typically ineffective because in general the regulatory agency lacks legally and politically defensible information on the polluter's abatement options, and because polluters have such strong incentives to delay compliance that the enforcement resources of the regulatory agency are overtaxed. To remedy these inherent defects and be effective, a regulatory agency would need such vast amounts of authority and manpower that a very different political system would be necessary.

Direct regulation is most workable when abatement technologies are fully known, when there are few polluters, and where no discharges whatever are allowed. The more closely these criteria are met, the more effective effluent standards are likely to be. Direct regulation is necessary—because indirect strategies such as charges are infeasible—when risks to public health are high (as in the case of toxic substances) and in general when the costs of monitoring are high. It is least desirable, and least likely to be effective, when abatement technologies are not fully known and when there are many sources of environmental damage. Yet these distinctions, and the logic behind them, are not widely understood.

Charge proposals need to be aired in public forums where their advocates can engage their critics and provide the information and

---

[4] The best review of the literature on the behavior of regulatory agencies, and of various proposals for their reform, is Roger Noll's *Reforming Regulation* (Washington, Brookings Institution, 1971).

opportunity for policymakers to think through the relative merits of charges and direct regulation. This may sound like the unhelpful counsel that in order for charges to get on the agenda they need to get on the agenda.[5] However, if charges are to become a feasible policy option, it will be only because of the slow but steady growth of organized advocates of charges and the economic research done in the past decade.

Support for Charges

Practical proposals for environmental charges require much applied economic and technical research to make them workable in specific contexts and to minimize undesirable secondary consequences. One of the factors responsible for charges finding more acceptance among persons interested in policy is the refinement in basic concepts and persuasive advocacy by proponents of charges in the 1960s. An early influence was *Managing Water Quality,* by Kneese and Bower; many of its concepts found their way into Senator William Proxmire's initial 1968 proposal for a regional basin charge system.

The second factor accounting for charges' increasing acceptance is the natural ally that the concept found among academically influenced government economists. To economists, the charge approach is such an obvious method of controlling pollution, one that cuts across liberal and conservative ideological orientations in the profession, that it took strong arguments about the strategy's supposed technical, administrative, and political defects to dissuade them. The charge approach first gained support in the Council of Economic Advisors, and then was taken up by other economist-influenced groups in Treasury, Bureau of the Budget, the Council on Environmental Quality, and the U.S. Environmental Protection Agency. This professional bias cannot be overlooked in explaining its frequent rebirth.

Until 1971, environmental organizations either took no stand on the issue or were hostile to a charge approach. At that time, however, President Nixon was convinced of the superiority of a charge approach over the existing regulatory system, and proposed a tax

---

[5] The politics of policy initiation in Congress are surveyed in Nelson Polsby, "Policy Analysis and Congress," *Public Policy* vol. 18 (Fall 1969) pp. 61–74.

on sulfur oxide emissions.[6] As a result, the major environmental organizations started to change their minds. Pollution charges are now supported by the Sierra Club, the National Audubon Society, and other environmental organizations of national importance.[7] There is even an environmental lobbying group called the Coalition to Tax Pollution.

This growth in support by organized groups is a significant, or potentially significant, change from the early 1970s when the major pollution control legislation was being passed. Charges may now have finally obtained enough political support to avoid being dismissed as an impractical proposal that even environmentalists support only lukewarmly. Interestingly, the charge concept is now getting favorable notice from some industry groups. Study committees of the National Association of Manufacturers and the Committee for Economic Development have come out in favor of the general polluter-pays principle and experiments with charges systems. It is still too early, however, to tell under what conditions industry in general would support a charge system.

The developments cataloged here make it more likely that when environmental policies are reevaluated, charges will be considered as a serious policy option. But even if the use of economic incentives is proposed at the next opportunity, charges will still face many political obstacles.

Misconceptions About Charges

A major obstacle to initial acceptance of the basic charge approach is the enormous misunderstanding surrounding the concept itself.

[6] See also J. Clarence Davies 3d, *The Politics of Pollution* (New York, Pegasus, 1970) pp. 177–179; Larry Ruff, "The Economic Common Sense of Pollution," *Public Interest* (Spring 1970) pp. 69–85; A. Myrick Freeman III, and Robert H. Haveman, "Clean Rhetoric and Dirty Water," *Public Interest* (Summer 1972) no. 28, pp. 54–65; and John F. Burby, "Environmental Report," *National Journal* October 21, 1972, pp. 1643–50 and October 28, pp. 1663–71, this being an account of the positions and maneuvers of those involved in the controversy over the Nixon administration's sulfur oxides tax proposal.

[7] For the environmentalists' turnabout, see *Economic Analysis and the Efficiency of Government. Part 6: Economic Incentives to Control Pollution.* Hearings before the Subcommittee on Priorities and Economy in Government of the Joint Economic Committee (92 Cong., 1 sess.) The testimony on July 12 and 19, 1971, contains the environmentalists' views.

This is revealed throughout the congressional testimony on charges. No doubt many of the misconceptions and confusions of the general public and the politicians stem from sheer unfamiliarity with a novel and complicated policy issue. Then, too, some confusion arises from the multiplicity of charge systems possible, and the characteristics of some of the initial plans.

Different proponents often have different objectives and rationales in mind when they put forward charge schemes. It would be too simple to say that the economist, administrator, and lawyer each views a charge as the solution to his own profession's problems in environmental policy, but there are clearly three different rationales: *cost effectiveness, administrative effectiveness,* and *equity.*

Using the cost effectiveness rationale, a charge system can be designed to allow interfirm marginal adjustments of pollution control that can achieve a given level of ambient quality at much smaller total costs to the firm and society than can direct regulation. While direct regulation may sometimes achieve cost effectiveness, it is by accident rather than design.

The administrative effectiveness of charges lies in the greater ease of enforcing compliance with abatement goals.

The equity objective is important because direct regulation is unfair in that some individuals are able to use environmental resources for free while passing on the costs of such use to others. Charges, by making every polluter pay an equal amount of "rent" per marginal pound of environmental resource used, thus equalize the burdens on polluters. Another equity argument is that because of the inevitably politically tainted pressures associated with direct regulation, the actual enforcement of standards is erratic and arbitrary, with only a few polluters being prosecuted for violations. This inequity can be eliminated by a charge system because of its greater effectiveness in enforcement.

It is important to remember these distinctions because the proponents of different charge plans often do not realize that they are disagreeing over different objectives and that there are tradeoffs among the three different goals. Often one objective can be maximized only at the expense of the other two.

One particular misconception warrants extended consideration. Many officials who have considered charges have said that they were unacceptable either because the charges would be a "license

to pollute," or because the public would believe they were. By "license to pollute" these officials mean that a firm could continue to pollute "legally" as long as it paid the charge. In the classical version of the effluent charge strategy this is perfectly true, but the rhetoric is misleading. Even the direct regulation approach presently used allows some discharges to continue, namely, any amount below the level of the standard. Above a certain concentration, discharges are illegal; below that point, discharges are "legal." In the same phraseology, firms have a license to pollute below the standards set for plant effluents in their locality. What is apparently unacceptable, however, is that individual polluters seem to have the choice of paying the charge and continuing to pollute; this is extrapolated into the fear that pollution levels in the region will be increased. A closer examination of the debate over the "license to pollute" is instructive. It reveals some important misconceptions about how a pollution charge system might operate.

The statement that firms which pay the charge can continue to pollute (under the classical or pure charge plan, that is) is often transformed into the prediction or conviction that firms will in fact pay the charge and continue as though nothing had changed. In economic theory, if the charge is set so that it is equal to or greater than the marginal costs of abatement (to the desired level) for a firm, the firm will try to reduce its discharges in order to save money and increase its profits, if it acts rationally as a cost-minimizing organization. But there are both sound and unsound criticisms of this formulation. The latter derive from a common failure to understand the marginal cost logic of modern economics. The former, although sometimes poorly articulated in the analytical terminology of economists, are usually different ways of framing the question: Will firms act rationally as assumed? Thus, in congressional hearings, one senator asked whether General Motors might not decide to pay the charge instead of reducing its emissions because the charge is such a "much smaller percentage of their costs of operation by reason of volume"?[8] And another

---

[8] These quotations are taken from the Hearings before the Subcommittee on Air and Water Pollution of the Senate Committee on Public Works, *Water Pollution—1970. Part I* (91 Cong., 2 sess.) See especially pp. 233, 240, 387. See also the *Congressional Record*, November 2, 1971, pp. S17426–433, for the floor colloquy between Muskie and Proxmire over the merits and demerits of Proxmire's river basin charge proposal.

senator asked whether an existing firm of marginal size and technology in its own industry might not prefer to pay the charge and
pollute rather than incur the capital costs of building a new plant
or the capital and operating costs of extremely costly abatement
facilities for an old plant, "even though the effluent charge is
geared realistically to the cost of cleaning up the effluent. . . ?"
These are not unintelligent questions when considered in their
contexts, and economists should be able to give satisfactory answers that support the charge approach. Yet the debate also includes a great deal of nonsense that passes without effective challenge and that poses a serious political liability for proponents of
charges. This is to be expected of a complicated innovation going
through the policy-making process.

Unlike the debate on the supersonic transport, in which a broad
consensus among congressional staff on the technical issues has
helped opponents, the complexities of the charge strategy have not
yet been digested by legislative aides. Until the assumptions and
doubts about charges are made explicit, reassuring answers will be
hard to frame. Once the need is evident, economists can enu-
merate the relatively few situations in which cost-minimizing
motivation may be insufficient, and ways to compensate, if desired, may be developed for such deficiencies. Once the issue of
whether profit-seeking behavior can be relied upon to induce firms
to reduce their emissions is settled, and the complexities are shown
to be manageable, the public debate can address the politically
more important and difficult questions that underlie the economic
motivation issue.

Affected Interest Groups

Congressional Oversight Committees

At present, the congressional committees that would have to ap-
prove a charge program at the federal level are cool toward the
charge concept. This resistance stems from both the particular industry interests affected by a charge proposal and the vested interests of those who oversee the present direct regulation system.

Senator Edmund Muskie's Subcommittee on Air and Water Pollution of the Senate Public Works Committee has had primary jurisdiction over the air and water pollution programs. He and his staff are very unsympathetic toward the charge approach. Economists have heavily criticized Senator Muskie's water control legislation and have proposed charges as a superior policy, so that in defense of his own record he is hostile to both those economists and their competing ideas. He is also worried that a charge program, because it would inevitably involve the taxation committees, would challenge his committee's heretofore almost exclusive jurisdiction over pollution control policy. Such a sharing of jurisdiction would, it is thought, reduce his committee's powers as well as endanger the viability of the pollution control programs. Proponents of a charge program have tried to design a plan that would make charges a supplement, not a substitute for the existing policies, thus protecting this committee's jurisdiction, but the Senator and his staff have been unmoved.

The House Ways and Means Committee is no more congenial to a pollution charge program, and there are strong doubts that a charge program could pass without its approval. This is because, if the House Ways and Means Committee insists on exercising its jurisdiction, it probably could not be circumvented even by a charge proposal that was artfully labeled a pollution "charge" or "fee" or "rent" rather than a "tax." In the past, the committee leadership has taken the public stance that the tax system should be used only to raise revenue, and not to control social behavior. Privately, the leadership is more pragmatic, looking at the countervailing political pressures that a charge proposal might generate, and insisting that a charge proposal be politically approvable. When Congressman Wilbur Mills was chairman, and the Nixon administration sent up its sulfur oxides tax proposal, industry had a virtual veto, and because of industry opposition the administration could find no Republican member of the committee willing to sponsor its bill. Under Chairman Al Ullman, the committee reported out a bill to tax new automobiles according to their gasoline consumption in order to create market incentives for the design and sale of more efficient automobiles; even though these parts of this energy conservation measure did not survive the floor fight, it may indicate a greater openness to using the tax system to deal with other environmental problems.

Regulatory Agencies

In the past, state pollution control agencies have shared with their federal counterparts a commitment to the direct regulation approach, and have been hostile both to the radical change implied by the pure charge system and to the major disruption a supplementary charge plan would entail.[9] While recently this attitude has begun to change, and important differences exist between federal and state agencies and among state agencies, the basic factors behind this aversion to charges are worth examining.

First, agency personnel are used to working with standards enforced by direct regulation, while effluent charges are a new and uncertain program. The agency people usually have had a difficult time achieving whatever they have accomplished and are understandably reluctant to start the process over again under different ground rules. They think that a charge system will require more stringent monitoring procedures than are now in use, and doubt their feasibility. Even when examining the monitoring procedures that might be used under different charge proposals, they tend to search for ways to "play the regulatory game"—to seek accommodations that would keep the regulated firms pacified and thus make life easier for the agency.

There is no realistic consideration of what life would be like for the agencies under the most politically feasible charge systems, for agency people seem convinced by assumption that either the direct regulation approach will work or nothing will. They counsel a "don't rock the boat" attitude. They know that any effective environmental charge proposal will be strongly resisted by industry, and probably by their agency's legislative supporters as well, and these political facts of life more than offset whatever theoretical attractions a charge strategy might have. Agency planners sometimes admit in private that they are not making a dramatic dent in pollution problems, and that, barring a series of technological miracles, will not meet even the now postponed deadlines. But given the exasperating problems involved in enforcement, and especially the painful conflict at the state level between environ-

---

[9] The only on-the-record collection of arguments against a charge proposal by a state regulatory agency that we are aware of, though it is no doubt dated now, is that by a Pennsylvania official in the hearings before the Proxmire subcommittee cited in footnote 7, pp. 1299–1300.

mental and economic development goals, they believe they are making as much progress as can reasonably be expected. They have a long list of ways to improve their programs, if only their legislatures would grant them new authority and additional staff and funding.

Finally, whereas charges have received some support at the federal level from economists in policy-making positions, there are few economists in the U.S. Environmental Protection Agency and even fewer in the state agencies. Since the regulatory agencies are staffed predominantly by engineers and lawyers, not only are there no inside advocates for a charge approach, but the charge idea must be sold to people with uncongenial professional outlooks. Engineers, especially the sanitary engineers who tend to dominate state agencies, do not think in terms of the economic motives and incentive structures facing a polluter, but instead think in terms of the engineering possibilities and technical solutions that are best fitted to the pollution problems the agency must deal with. Lawyers in the regulatory agencies also have their professional bias. They are accustomed to working within the confines of existing laws, rather than thinking about the most theoretically desirable policies for a particular problem. They therefore tend to have a narrow view of the legal tools and purposes of regulating economic enterprises, and to lag behind the thinking of the more policy-oriented lawyers in the law schools. For example, they often take their notions of "equity" from areas that are strangers to the economic motivations of the pollution field. Lacking the economists' inbred notion of the appropriateness of "rent" for scarce environmental, or common property resources, or the importance of economic incentives in encouraging research into better abatement alternatives, these lawyers not infrequently view a charge as inequitable: after all, they reason, if a polluter has no feasible abatement option, putting a tax on his discharges in order to reduce them is unfair because the polluter has no ability to avoid breaking the law.

These various professional biases result in a misunderstanding of the nature and purposes of a pollution charge system and powerfully constrain the receptiveness of the existing environmental control agencies to a charge system, and especially to a charge system promoted by economists. They make it more likely that a charge proposal will be forced upon a regulatory agency

from without, against its passive or active opposition, than be initially promoted by the agency.

More optimistically, this conclusion may underestimate the learning that may go on in the regulatory agencies as they gain experience with direct regulation, for these agencies may become more favorably disposed to charges as the threat of embarrassing failure with direct enforcement of standards grows more likely. As the deadlines for compliance with standards loom nearer, the inability of many polluters to meet them may also become more obvious. A regulatory agency may then search for strategies that do not place it in the politically embarrassing situation of enforcing sanctions that are too harsh to be credible, or letting the polluters continue to violate the standards. Pollution control agencies may search for "graduated response" strategies that are both effective and credible. Just such foreboding thoughts have occurred to some government policy makers concerned with what they see as the coming crunch in the automobile emissions standards program. If the automobile manufacturers cannot meet the (now postponed) deadlines, is EPA going to fine them $10,000 per car, effectively shutting them down? No one seriously believes this could happen, yet EPA has no other sanction available. A charge nicely avoids the necessity to make such tortuous "yes/no" choices. By making the question in 1977 (now 1979) one of whether the auto companies were charged $115 or $60 for every car that exceeded the emissions standard, rather than whether General Motors production should be shut down because its emission control devices were 80 percent effective rather than the required 90 percent, a charge scheme can avoid the deadline problem entirely. Thus, "post-deadline charges"—charges on those polluters who fail to meet specified timetables and who appear to need an extra inducement—may become acceptable as the presently available sanctions appear to be ineffective or worse than the problems they are designed to eliminate.

Industry

The strongest and most predictable opposition to the introduction of a charge system will come from the affected industries.[10] This

---

[10] Not all polluters are private profit-making firms, of course. Municipalities are

opposition derives from a quite rational calculation that industry is likely to be better off under the present system than under a charge system. Even though the average firm will pay less to reach a given ambient standard under a charge system than under a system of direct regulation that approximates uniform percentage reductions in discharges, the real basis of comparison must take into consideration the probability of having to comply. Under a charge system, a firm is almost certain to have to pay the charge, or spend money to abate in order to reduce its charge payments. Under direct regulation, however, an industry might conclude that because the enforcement mechanisim is so cumbersome and ineffective, it either will not have to pay for the most expensive kinds of abatement techniques, or will be able to gain the monetary advantages of years of delay past the official deadlines. Thus, all other factors being equal, the firm, in rational self-interest, would prefer the present system to an effective charge system.

The situation is made slightly more complicated, however, by the alternatives industry believes it faces. The present system of direct regulation has other costs and uncertainties that bother businessmen. It is more costly than charges, but with the problems it has in enforcement, it cannot be easily modified to take advantage of various cost-reducing strategies. It is erratic and capricious, as effluent standards are subject to new interpretations, as some violators but not others are prosecuted, as the fads of public attention lead to "on-again–off-again" pressures on the agency to produce visible successes. Direct regulation also intrudes into corporate privacy, for determining practicable abatement technol-

---

especially important in water pollution and solid waste disposal. And municipalities are no more eager to raise taxes to pay for abatement facilities or to pay a pollution charge than is a private firm. They are a potent political force as well, but since many industrial polluters dump their effluent into municipal sewage systems, and since municipalities are in their own right significant polluters, a charge on the important water pollutants should apply to public as well as private polluters. There are two difficulties with this. First, public policy may be more sensitive to the plight of economically marginal towns in raising funds for abatement and charge payments than to that of private firms.

Second, federal policy has been to subsidize the construction of municipal wastewater treatment plants, with the result that localities do not begin construction until they are sure of receiving federal approval, and hence funds. Thus, a charge on municipal wastes would probably have to include a grace period to take into account delay "caused" by delay in the federal approval process.

ogies means that a regulatory agency must consider such factors as the availability of capital, profit rates, accounting practices that might hide true profits, and research and development decisions of a firm, as well as the efficiency of available technologies.

On the other hand, industry is dissatisfied with the present air and water quality standards, and the debate over switching to such an economics-oriented system as charges might well provide an opportunity for reevaluating the benefits and costs of the goals of direct regulation. Finally, it is also in the interest of industry to have the pollution problem "solved" so that industry is no longer widely perceived as a villain in American politics; a more efficient, equitable, and effective system of pollution control is a means to that end. For these and other reasons, industry is not as united against pollution charges today as it was in 1972, when congressional hearings on pollution charges were last held, and might be more open to some kinds of charge plans in the future. Publicly, however, industry representatives have made three main arguments against charges.

THE "DOUBLE BURDEN" ARGUMENT. One of the most potent political arguments that industry is likely to make is the claim that paying the charge takes away money industry would otherwise be able to spend on pollution control. This claim has a strong surface validity, but is based on assumptions that should be inspected. Certainly, if polluters were making every effort to invest in the abatement technologies necessary to achieve air and water quality standards by the publicly set deadlines, it would be unnecessary to switch from the present system for enforcement reasons (although it would still make sense in terms of economic efficiency). This assumption of eager and willing compliance is not, in fact, a realistic description. But the real question is, even though many firms are not acting in ways that will achieve the desired standards on time, will a charge tend to hamper their now-insufficient efforts or will it prod them into more vigorous efforts to comply?

In evaluating the double burden argument, one must distinguish the theoretical possibility that a charge will be applied in full the first year of a pollution control program from the more realistic situation in which a charge is imposed gradually over a period of years, or takes effect near the deadlines for the achieve-

ment of the ambient standards. If the charge were imposed in full at the start of an abatement program, that is, with little warning and no grace period for polluters to reduce their discharges before the charge became effective, then there is little that a firm could do, even at its best, to reduce its charge payments in the first year or so. It takes time for a firm to analyze its abatement possibilities, design or decide on new equipment, and purchase, construct, and de-bug the new technology. Of course, the lead time would vary, with some firms able to reduce their emissions significantly in a six-month period while others would require several years of intensive research and development to find out which abatement technologies would be worth full-scale tests on their plants. Given the lead times involved, then, a charge applied at more than nominal levels the first few years would be a "double burden" in the restricted sense that there may be no reasonable action that a firm could take to reduce its charge payments.

A firm is not likely to find itself in this situation. Enactment of charge legislation will take time, and charge systems with a serious chance of passage will undoubtedly have a schedule which increases over time from a quite nominal "attention-getting" level to a final higher level. Thus firms will find themselves subject to a relatively higher charge only after several years, during which time they presumably will have invested in abatement controls or will have had time to complete research on more effective control techniques. In this sense, then, they will have been given an opportunity to avoid what they term "double payment." Firms that do not take advantage of this grace period are precisely those firms that require the additional incentive of a charge to induce them to abate.

THE "SMALL FIRM" ARGUMENT.   Congressional testimony indicates a great sensitivity to the allegation that a charge would have a disproportionately adverse impact on small firms compared with large and diversified corporations.[11] Basically, this argument assumes that one or more of the following propositions are true and significant: There are significant economies of scale in abatement techniques and in general, abatement costs are likely to be large

[11] See, for example, the hearings before the Muskie subcommittee cited in footnote 8, Part I, pp. 198 and 240.

relative to revenue or profits. Small firms are less profitable or less efficient than larger firms in the same industry; are less diversified so that they cannot use tax credits to offset the costs of abatement for one product with profits from another product; are less capable of passing the costs of abatement forward to their customers; generally have less access to outside capital than larger firms; are less likely to have adequate research and development resources available to deal with abatement problems and, even if they do, have a smaller revenue base upon which to amortize their research and development expenditures.

Some of these propositions are true. The first question, however, concerns their significance. In absolute terms, are small firms unable to find abatement options that are as efficient as those of larger firms, and are abatement costs actually a large part of the firm's costs? We now know that these facts vary considerably from industry to industry, and we now have better data on which to base an answer than we did just a few years ago. But more importantly, it is often forgotten in the debate that small firms are also disadvantaged under the present program. The relevant base for comparison is not between charges and no pollution control program whatever, but between charges and direct regulation. Small firms complain at present that they are disadvantaged in various way. There is an overrepresentation of large firms on the technical advisory panels that help set industry effluent standards, often because large firms can afford to have their engineers spend time on such panels and on gathering backup evidence. The technology-based effluent standards these panels suggest thus may tend to favor the abatement possibilities open only to large plants. On another level, since smaller firms lack the political, legal, and technical resources of larger firms, they are easier targets for regulatory agencies trying to convince the public that they are pursuing their goals aggressively.

If Congress is worried about the differential impacts of an effective pollution control program on small firms, the charge system provides a more flexible policy for dealing with the problem. Given an adequate criterion to distinguish small from large firms in an industry, smaller firms could be assigned a smaller charge level, or probably more preferably, would have to meet the normal charge level several years after the large firms. This would give

them extra time in which to spread out their research and capital expenditures and would put them in a better position to take advantage of the intervening years' research on abatement done by the more closely pressed larger firms in their industry and in the field of abatement technology generally.

Special exemptions for small firms, at least initially, would also be an easy way to reduce the opposition of a sizable and politically vociferous interest group, while attending to the relatively large firms which often account for the largest absolute share of total discharges.[12] Many other public policies exempt small firms from coverage, often on the straightforward cost–benefit grounds that the costs of administering or reporting are too great relative to the possible benefits. In any case, as with the extension of the minimum wage law to cover smaller and smaller firms in more and more industries, a charge system could achieve full coverage by stages rather than by first application.

Institutional Design Issues

Length of Imposition

Charge system designers face a choice: Should the charges apply only until the ambient standards in a region have been achieved, or should they be continuous and apply even after the ambient quality goals have been met? The plan to charge until standards are met was incorporated into the Nixon administration's sulfur oxides tax proposal, but the continuous charge is the version supported by practically all economists.

The argument in favor of charging until standards are met is that once the ambient goals have been achieved, polluters should no longer have to pay. After all, this reasoning goes, since ambient goals are set to balance social costs and benefits, or to reach levels at which there are no health and property damages, discharges below the ambient levels are not damaging and therefore should be free. If Congress or the EPA wants a higher ambient standard,

---

[12] In the early years, it was EPA policy to go after the big sources first, more or less ignoring the numerous small ones since 5–10 percent of all firms account for 50–90 percent of all pollution. *Environmental Law Reporter* vol. 1, p. 10138.

as continuation of the charge implies, then it should be made explicit and the stricter standard justified.

This kind of argument is basically a misunderstanding of how charges work. *A charge is imposed not only to achieve the ambient goals but also to maintain them.* If the charge is taken off when the ambient standards are achieved, firms will no longer have an incentive to continue operating their abatement processes. This would result in oscillatory behavior, and produce great uncertainty, as firms reacted to the cessation of charges by increasing discharges, only to have the charges reimposed as the ambient standards deteriorate. In a steady-state economy, with no new firms entering the area, and no additions to plant capacity or changes in production technology or inputs, such a system might work; once the charge had achieved the ambient goal, the regulatory agency would simply monitor every plant's discharges and not allow them to exceed the amounts set at the time the ambient standards were first achieved. But such a world exists only in fiction; in the real world such a system would lead to all the problems that now plague direct regulation.[13]

Regulation, whether standards or charges, usually amplifies inequities because it tends to use uniform rules. Uniform rules, because they apply to parties in slightly different initial circumstances, inevitably affect the parties differentially, forcing some to bear heavier burdens than others. Yet, administratively uniform rules are easier to promulgate and enforce. The result is that, in exchange for the ability to use uniform rules, a regulatory agency in a political context in which the regulated are both influential

---

[13] The drafters of the Nixon administration's SO_x tax foresaw this difficulty, and sought to mitigate it by having the charge decrease slowly, with the charge rate for any given year after the standard had been achieved being calculated on the base of the *previous* year so that there would be at least a one-year time lag to dampen oscillatory behavior. They also assumed that linear programming models would be used by polluters or the agency in the area to enforce "tacit norms" for emissions after the charge was completely removed. New firms were to be permitted to bring into the region the "pollution quota" they had had in their old region, to be applied against their new charge. But the designers agreed informally that this plan was analogous to the risky medical practice of administering an extremely toxic but beneficial drug, and then giving its antidote a short time later, in the hope that the beneficial effects would start working but that the antidote would work quickly enough to inhibt the toxic side effects. To be sure, this is successful sometimes, but it requires both great skill and complex controls over possible disturbing influences —both of which are likely to be lacking in a real-world charge system.

and required to bear heavy costs usually has to have either "loop-holes" or an explicit "exemptions" process. Loopholes allow people to cheat and in safety-valve fashion thus save the regulatory agency from the political pressures generated by a policy that drives the regulated parties to the wall (or to Congress); an exemptions process more formally takes into consideration the different initial circumstance and realistic options of some of those affected by the policy.

Charges and direct regulation systems differ in their capacity for formal and informal exemptions. A system of direct regulation of standards has many points—indeed, too many points—at which its theoretically burdensome impacts can be mitigated in practice: setting standards at a low level, selective enforcement of the official standards, and formal variances. A charge, on the other hand, is more easily made into an administrative automaton, with little informal discretion in enforcement. Thus under a charge system, exemptions and variances must be granted formally, meaning publicly, with standard rules and explicit and defensible justifications. This may be looked upon by some politicians and agencies as undesirable, for some presently granted exemptions could not be well justified publicly, and making public the magnitude of the exemptions that are granted *de facto* through the deficiencies of the present standard-setting and enforcement process might well be embarrassing.

On the other hand, charges have a distinct advantage over direct regulation in the issue of variances. When an agency operates with direct regulation (or with a low charge), it is difficult for the agency to publicly grant exemptions and variances without seeming to favor polluters. No matter how unfair or inaccurate this image may be, it may measurably restrict the freedom of the agency to grant exemptions for reasonable cases. It is not only the agency's public image that controls its actions; the agency itself will always have doubts about the real motivations and truthfulness of the polluters to which it grants exemptions. However, when an agency works with a moderate or relatively strong charge, it is less constrained by its own real and imagined fears and the possible damage to its public image. It is more willing to give exemptions in hardship cases because it and the public recognize that the charge alone is acting as a strong inducement in the right direction.

Variations in the Charge Schedule

While our discussion has generally assumed that charges will be nationally uniform—the same charge for the same pollutant over the entire area to be covered—it is not the only possible or perhaps even desirable type of charge. Three classes of variations have frequently been proposed in place of a uniform national charge. They are regional charges, charges that take into account the variation in the assimilative capacity of the receiving medium, and charges that vary according to economic impact on different industries. Each variant has been championed by some economists and industrialists because each reduces the economic resources that must be invested to achieve a given level of environmental quality. Thus each in some way reduces the costs borne by polluters, public or private, and sometimes by regions as a whole. On the other hand, there are often other costs in attempting to reduce the direct costs borne by industry. In this case, the costs are generally public costs such as increased administrative cumbersomeness that may reduce the effectiveness of the pollution control program, and sometimes greater political difficulty in reaching agreement on a charge plan. The latter kinds of costs are usually not investigated, especially the political costs of greater complexity, but these potential political and political–administrative costs deserve our attention.

REGIONAL VERSUS UNIFORM NATIONAL CHARGES.   If a pollution charge is regional in coverage—varying for different regions of the country or a state, however "region" is defined—then the first political problem is that there may be industrial relocation, with possible adverse effects on both the old and new locations. Differences in charges among regions will be an incentive for firms to move from regions of relatively high charges to regions of relatively low charges. The regional authorities will realize this and (especially if they set the charge themselves) seek to underbid each other to attract new industries or avoid losing old ones, nullifing the effectiveness of the charge system in achieving the ambient standards.

On the other hand, if the charge is uniform over the entire country, industries will not change their sites but the outcome of

pollution reduction efforts will be different for different regions.
In general, this would tend to make the relatively clean regions
much purer than the standards require while the relatively dirty
regions are brought barely up to the standards. Politically, the
problem with a uniform (continuous) national charge is that the
clean regions will complain that they are being forced to pay more
for abatement than would be necessary to reach their regional
standards or the national minimum. This is because the initial
charge is likely to be set so as to make sure that the relatively polluted regions are at least made tolerably clean within a reasonable
time. Why should the relatively clean regions bear this added cost?
One reason given, by no means the only or the most important
one, is that the relatively dirty areas, which are mainly urban and
highly industrialized, would lose industry and jobs to the cleaner
regions if they had to pay full pollution costs. This is equivalent
to saying that the dirty regions do not want to pay for their environmental benefits in the currency of lost industry and jobs.

Some environmentalists' objections to regionally differentiated
charges stem not only from a desire to retain a uniform national
charge's administrative advantages, but also from the high value
placed on a "nondegradation" policy. That is, in pristine areas the
quality of the environment should not be degraded to ambient
standards. A continuous uniform charge prevents this from hap-
pening because it removes the incentive of polluters to move to the
relatively clean regions, with their lower ambient concentrations
and lower charge levels. A straightforward effort to ensure that the
air and water of the relatively pure regions is not degraded to the
minimum national standards could defuse some of the environmentalists' oppositions to regional variations.

The most important reason for preferring a uniform charge,
however, is the political difficulty of deciding upon the charges for
different regions. It will be hard enough to decide on the national
charge for a given pollutant, the industries or other sources to be
covered, and the relation of different pollutants to each other
without the added burden of predicting the location effects of a
charge that varies from region to region, and of either setting the
regional charges or deciding on the structure and procedures of the
regional charge-setting institutions. As pointed out below, charges
are calculated on the basis of rather imperfect data, and the more

imperfect the information, the greater the suspicion that the different regional charge levels have been set by a political process that favors one region's economy over another's.

How might the political problems that arise from either a regional or a uniform charge be reduced or eliminated? Consider the competitive industrial location effects of a regional charge plan. There is first of all the question of how significant, in fact, these effects might be. After all, pollution control costs are only one element among many that must be considered when a plant site is chosen. Many industries are bound to their local or regional markets and really have little choice. Other industries with a multi-regional or national market have more locational options in theory, but probably only in highly unusual circumstances would the differences in regional abatement costs counterbalance the other considerations that lead a firm to locate in a certain region. Nevertheless, it would be politically useful to obtain and present hard data showing the magnitude and specific effects of a uniform charge.

The fear of location effects might be eased or eliminated completely by a special surcharge on new plants analogous to the special national emission standards for "new sources" of air pollution. Such a surcharge would equalize the charge among regions for all new sources. Special standards or charges for new plants make sense because it is usually far easier to design efficient abatement techniques into a new plant before it is built than to try to install them in an existing plant. With a higher and equalizing charge on new plants, the incentive of firms to move from a region with a relatively high charge to a region with a relatively low charge would be eliminated.

Some opposition to regionally varied charges reflects an estimate that if the charges are set by state or regional authorities, they will be too low practically everywhere to have much environmental effectiveness. A "minimum" charge calculated to achieve the national ambient standards in many, but not all, regions might eliminate this objection. The relatively polluted regions would have the obligation of deciding on surcharges to meet ambient standards, but at least an effective floor would have been set below which they could not go. If at some later date the dirty regions were remiss in their efforts, a special surcharge could be specified for them. The advantage of this approach is that once a working

charge system is in place, it is much easier to affect the overall
effectiveness of the system by raising the charge than it is to try to
increase the tools and motivations of the state and federal agencies
which must enforce standards directly.

Another way to overcome the problems of deciding the different
charge levels is the "self-setting charge," which automatically increases by a certain amount annually until a region's ambient
standard is achieved, at which point it either becomes constant or
automatically decreases by a certain amount each year until the
ambient standards begin to be imperiled again. Thus if legislators
thought that a charge of 10¢ per pound of BOD was an effective
charge level nationally for practically all industries, they might set
the charge schedule to begin at 2¢ per pound the first year, with
2¢ increments until the 10¢ level had been reached in five years,
followed by a 1¢ increment annually for each year that the standard had not been met in each region, or by a 1¢ decrement for
each year that the standard had been met.

If a clean region achieved ambient standards in three years, its
polluters would pay only 6¢ per pound, and if the ambient levels
improved the following year, only 5¢. By allowing the charge to
find its own level, the political and technical difficulties of deciding on the various regional charges would be eliminated.

The major objection is that the uncertainty about the ultimate
level of the charge will lead to fluctuations in pollution levels.
According to this argument, firms with relatively high abatement
costs might calculate that if all the other firms react to what they
believe will be an eventual charge level of 10¢, the ambient standards will actually be achieved at 8¢. A firm with average abatement costs of 10¢ that thought this might decide to react to the
charge as if it would only be 8¢ and not build abatement facilities.
If enough firms did this, they could all be proved wrong by their
own actions. The charge level might in fact rise to 12¢ as firms
slowly came to realize they had misjudged each other. Then an expanded abatement effort might overshoot the standards considerably. This scenario is a familiar one in economics. In the present
case, however, it assumes the improbable—that no firm or agency
in a charge region would construct a simulation model to give
everyone a relatively good idea of the effects of different ultimate

charge levels on the ambient standards, so that a rational informal goal could be set.

The foregoing stratagems help eliminate some of the political problems associated with regional charges, but uniform charges may still be preferable. There are no clever charge system designs that will eliminate the objections of the relatively clean regions to unnecessary costs, without doing violence to the overall effectiveness of the charge system. However, there is no point in trying to work out a complicated regional system if the differential impacts of a uniform national charge are not very significant. These differences may well vary according to the pollutant and the affected industry, and if the designers of the initial charge system wanted to avoid regional uncertainties in administration by having a uniform national charge, a pollutant that had little differential regional impacts could be chosen. The first requirement, again, would seem to be specific information on the different costs of abatement that characterize the clean and dirty regions.

CHARGES THAT VARY BY ASSIMILATIVE CAPACITY. Congressional attitudes on incorporating the concept of assimilative capacity into the pollution control program are mixed. The 1970 Clean Air Act allows variations in the natural assimilative capacity of the atmosphere caused by meteorological conditions to be taken into account in determining effluent standards. On the other hand, the Federal Water Pollution Control Act Amendments of 1972 abandon the concept and call instead for a "no discharge" policy, apparently having concluded that the concept was administratively too cumbersome.

While the great advantage of a control strategy that uses variations in assimilative capacity is that it results in lower costs, the great disadvantage is that much more information is required in order to properly administer the strategy. It requires information on the assimilative capacity of a particular body of water or air under different conditions, and often continuous real-time monitoring to determine when these conditions change. Such data do not exist, with rare exceptions, and would likely take years to obtain. Yet if the savings to polluters were great enough to pay for the extra administrative staff, research, and monitoring that would

be required, there might be relatively simple and effective ways to couple a regional assimilative capacity system to either a regional or national charge system. For instance, this could be done by a system of rebates based on calculations of the effluents that were rendered harmless within a certain distance from the firm's outfalls, perhaps varying by time of year or day or even according to weather or river flow conditions.

Charges based on assimilative capacity can be used for air as well as water pollution control, but the political problems are more fundamental in the water area because the possibility of joint treatment facilities with significant economies of scale and the integration of nonpoint sources into the management program both imply an overarching institutional structure. A truly comprehensive regional river basin authority would have to deal with other issues in addition to setting a charge level that reached ambient standards; it would have to set standards for different stretches of a river and its tributaries, decide tradeoffs among different environmental goals, deal with recreational as well as pollution problems, coordinate its policies with the growth and land use of policies of the surrounding political jurisdictions, and decide what to do with its charge revenue.

As organizational theory demonstrates, different organizational structures tend to promote different questions for debate and decision, and to preshape the substantive policy outcomes. Moreover, in this case, the regional institution would not be set in an organizational vacuum but would have to be set up to mesh with existing local and state agencies and political jurisdictions. Since a regional arrangement that is effective is sure to upset existing power and privilege structures, both public and private, this is not a trivial task, as the history of efforts to set up regional institutions in this country attests. Charges could be instrumental in encouraging the formation of river basin authorities because the lure of reduced charge payments through an integrated river basin management plan is likely to be extremely attractive to municipal and industrial polluters. Thus the question will be what kinds of new regional institutions we wish to encourage, and what will be the consequences, political and environmental, of such institutions?[14]

---

[14] That the institutional dangers exist is attested by two examples. The first is an apparent attempt by polluting interests to subvert the individual states' air quality

The institutional problems of river basin authorities have spawned a separate and elaborate literature, to which the interested reader is directed.[15]

INDUSTRY-BY-INDUSTRY VARIATIONS. A potent political argument against a uniform charge will be that a proposed charge level for a pollutant would have intolerable effects on a firm or industry important to local, regional, or national economies. Barring outright exemption, the remedy, it will be said, is to charge these firms at a lower rate. For example, the charge level on SO_x that would increase the price of electricity by 10 percent while reducing SO_x emissions from fossil-fuel electric power plants by 90 percent, might also, in the absence of an effective abatement technology, make many nonferrous smelters uncompetitive with foreign producers. The figures in this example are hypothetical but the problem it highlights is not. If a firm or industry is fully exempted from the charge, then a program of direct regulation, with its particular liabilities of enforcement and lack of incentives for the polluter to do research, must be used instead. If, in order to avoid the choice between one charge rate for all and complete exemption, a series of special lower charges are created, an unfortunate precedent is set. The way is open for every industry to claim that it too deserves special treatment for its own problems, and for politically influential firms and industries to gain special treatment they do not deserve. The administrative and political problems of multiple charge rates for the same pollutant may be so severe that it is better to avoid such charges entirely.

Exemptions can still be granted, of course, but exemptions in the form of reduced charge rates may not be the best type. The political process may be able to handle time variations—the grant-

---

laws by setting up interstate compact agencies that are more likely to be influenced by industrial interests; this proposal was embodied in S.907 in 1971. The second danger is that of a regional agency becoming so independent by virture of its political and financial resources that it takes on a life of its own, as the New York–New Jersey Port Authority is often accused of having done. With the user charges from its joint treatment facilities as an assured source of financing, a river basin authority might constantly seek new ways to spend the excess funds collected, expanding into many other water-related but nonpollution abatement activities.

[15] For a comprehensive review of the institutional problems and possibilities of river basin authorities, see Marc J. Roberts, "Organizing Water Pollution Control:

ing of six-month or one- or two-year variances—more easily than variations in the charge level itself. This is because it is easier to relate a problem and time needed to remedy it to a particular time estimate than it is to figure out and agree on what charge reduction would be neither too much nor too little. If an electric power company, for example, claims it has not been able to find a source of moderately priced low-sulfur coal, and will not be able to either locate the coal or install stack gas equipment for a year, it is easier to say that it should be exempted for a year than it is to determine whether the charge should be reduced by, say, 33 percent or 67 percent. Possibly, too, time exemptions would be less likely to become permanent than reduced-charge exemptions. Once the time period is up, a firm or industry would have to go through the exemptions process again or be without the protection it claims it still needs and deserves. If the exemption were in the form of reduced charges, however, there might be less pressure on the administrative agency or the Congress to enforce the deadlines for the exemptions. The industry would claim that the lower charge was having some positive effect, so why not continue the status quo? Indeed, it may be desirable to create different exemption procedures, making greater exemptions proportionately harder to obtain—for example, as in the auto emissions field, allowing an administrative agency to grant variances up to one year in duration, but requiring that cumulative exemptions of more than two years have to go through the more difficult congressional clearance process.

Setting the Charge

CALCULATING THE CHARGE. The question of *how* a charge would be calculated is as much a political issue as the question of *who* would set the charge. The calculation of the charge remains a source of controversy, and doubts that a satisfactory method is available reduce the support for the charge strategy.

Politically, a technique for calculating the charge must satisfy two divergent criteria. On the one hand, it must be high enough

to provide a sufficient incentive for polluters to reduce their discharges by an amount that will achieve the desired ambient standards. On the other hand, it must not be higher than is necessary to reach the ambient standards, for then it is merely "punitive" and the higher charge buys mainly more closed plants and unemployed workers. In a phrase, it must be neither an "undercharge" nor an "overcharge."[16] Since an environmentalist's undercharge can be a polluter's overcharge, the calculation technique or the political process of setting the charge must somehow reconcile these opposing forces. Insofar as economists cannot come up with a calculus that seems rationally to arrive at the precise charge that will achieve a given ambient level within a specified time, congressmen must grapple with the charge decision according to other, less technical, criteria.

Basically, two different methods for setting the charge have been proposed. The first is based on the so-called "social damages" caused by pollution. The second involves setting the charge on the basis of abatement costs and using it to achieve ambient standards. The arguments against the theoretical appropriateness of basing charges on social damages are strong. Even those who support this method recognize that it is impractical at present and is likely to remain so for the forseeable future because we lack information on the full damages and the monetary costs and benefits of reducing environmentally caused damages. Politically, however, the theory that the charge should reflect the damages caused by pollution is so attractive as a weapon that it is hard to resist. Since estimates of property and health costs alone, leaving aside other damages less easily measured, are often higher than the cost of abatement (to reach the ambient standards), they are a handy polemical cudgel against those who complain about the costs and consequences of stringent environmental policies. Such estimates make more real the fact that polluters are imposing costs on other people in the form of property damage, poor health, and restricted recreational opportunities.

Social damage estimates tend to slant the public debate toward higher rather than lower charges, although the regional variations in damages that sophisticated studies reveal can backfire against

16 The phrase is from Orlando E. Delogu, "A State Approach to Effluent Charges," *Maine Law Review* vol. 23, no. 2 (1971) p. 283.

uniform national charge proposals. Thus EPA's estimate that the damages caused by sulfur dioxide nationally amount to 25¢ per pound was used by Treasury Department representatives in discussions with utility and coal industry officials to rebut complaints that the lower (20¢) charges proposed by Treasury were too burdensome and unjustifiable. Although it is hard to predict what the costs of sulfur dioxide abatement will be in the power industry, they are not likely to be as high as 25¢ per pound at high levels of efficiency; however, one appears to be making a concession in talking about any charge level below 25¢ per pound, and this is sometimes an important political advantage. Nevertheless, it is not a decisive political advantage, not only because politicians do not understand welfare economics, but because politicians are much more concerned with the distribution of costs and benefits among particular groups than they are with average costs.

Economists and politicians generally support the second charge calculation technique, that of setting the charge on the basis of the costs of abatement and using it to achieve ambient standards. This method is acceptable when the abatement techniques for a given pollutant and industry are known. When abatement alternatives do not seem to exist for a given pollutant and industry, the deficiencies in methodology and data lead to political problems.

When abatement techniques are known, there is sufficient information to calculate the effects of a charge of any given level. With data on the costs and effectiveness of abatement techniques, it is relatively easy to see at what charge level a firm will stop paying the charge and switch to a given abatement technique. Given information on how long it takes firms to implement an abatement plan once the charge level has reached the point where it becomes profitable to adopt a specific abatement technique, it is then possible to construct emission diffusion models and to calculate when the total discharges will reach to the ambient standards desired. With similar information, it is also possible to calculate the different economic impacts on various regions and industries, and the consequent political problems that might be expected. And if one believes that an effective charge will lead to advances in abatement technology, then a charge calculated even on the basis of presently known techniques will result in greater environmental improvement (or the same environmental goal at lesser

cost, depending on whether the polluter is allowed to capture the technological gains in the form of cost savings or has to pass them on to society in the form of increased environmental benefits). The assumption here is not of perfect information. The figures will be rough, but with them it will be possible to obtain a general idea of what the primary environmental and social impacts of various charges are likely to be. Politically this is probably satisfactory.

The problem arises when the data on cost of abatement are not very good. Does a charge system then become politically unworkable because the distributional impacts and probable environmental goals are highly uncertain? The costs of alternative cleaner technologies may not be known, for instance, simply because the technologies either have not been developed at all (a rare situation today, although a real problem some years ago), or are in such an early stage of development that cost and performance estimates are not reliably known (especially outside the industry). This is not a theoretical problem; the nonferrous smelter industry argues that no technically (by which they mean economically) feasible effective abatement method exists to treat their sulfur oxides emissions. In such a situation how might a legislature set the charge?

SETTING CHARGES WHEN INFORMATION IS LACKING. In situations of highly imperfect information, there are three general decision strategies that a legislature might employ. First, the legislature could decide the charge mainly on the basis of the pain it was willing to have the affected firms and regions endure, rather than on the basis of what a given charge would accomplish in reducing pollution. While an economist can accept this as an incentive to encourage otherwise lagging research on abatement techniques, or as a rent on common property resources, politicians are averse to not having a solid instrumental basis for setting a charge, or to penalizing someone for doing something that he has no feasible option to avoid. Thus, setting the charge with highly imperfect information is not likely to gain much political support—with one important exception. It may be much more acceptable to impose a roughly calculated charge on new plant sources, for those sources have more options than existing plants and are being designed under new rules.

A second strategy of decision might be termed the deferred pain strategy. Legislators may be more willing to set higher charges if they can use a charge that increases gradually over time to a maximum value. In this way the risk of immediate damages from a high charge is minimized, while firms without efficient abatement techniques are given a strong inducement to begin serious research immediately. Later, as the high charge begins to take effect, legislators may reason, they can act in time to ameliorate any undesirable or unanticipated consequences. Without knowing what the exact economic and environmental impacts will be, a legislature may well assume that a gradually increasing charge will stimulate technological innovations, and that after three or four years of charges the technological possibilities will have been much better explored and their costs demonstrated. At that time it will still be possible to make another decision on what tax rate will achieve the desired environmental goals, all things considered. This is the strategy adopted, *de facto,* by the Federal Water Pollution Control Act Amendments of 1972 with its sponsors' talk of a "midcourse correction."

Finally, a third way to deal with the political problems of charge setting in a situation of relatively soft data is to rely on an elaborate "exemptions" process to take care of the hardships an effective charge level is likely to produce. Such an exemptions process is part of the hedging or insurance strategies that a novel policy is likely to be encumbered with: those who fear overcharges opt for a flexible exemptions process; those who fear undercharges try to maintain a parallel system of regulatory control based on direct enforcement. Together they reduce the theoretical efficiency the charge system, standing alone, might have; but this may be the price to be paid for experimenting with a charge plan initially.

A basis for optimism is that information on abatement techniques is improving all the time. There are many industries that would still argue that they do not have "feasible" abatement options, but outside experts seem convinced that this is true for only a few and that the abatement costs for the major pollutants are now known within the requisite accuracy. On the continuum from "known" to "unknown" abatement techniques and costs, we are now arguing in the middle portion, and the political process can more easily handle debates there.

ALTERNATIVE CHARGE-SETTING ARRANGEMENTS.   The foregoing analysis of the technical basis for calculating the charge and the economic stakes involved in the charge decision makes it apparent how "political" the charge decision is likely to be. It is "political" not only in the sense that important distributional issues are inevitably affected, but also in the sense that the decision cannot be made only on the basis of scientific facts and methods, but must involve value choices at important points. This fact enhances our interest in the specific institutional arrangements for arriving at a charge schedule.

Underlying one's attitude toward a charge system in comparison with other approaches is a judgment about the politics of charge setting: Will it be politically feasible to achieve a charge high enough to be effective? In large part, of course, the answer depends on the political strength of those who favor more effective environmental policies, and no amount of ingenuity in designing a charge system can compensate for basic political weakness. But since political support and opposition depend on the precise features of a charge plan, and since there is great leeway in designing a charge plan to take into consideration specific organizational and distributional objections while still retaining some of the advantages of a charge approach, the political prospects for a charge plan clearly depend mainly on its specific features. Still, both in theory and intuitively, we know that the outcome of the charge decision also depends on what institutional arrangements are devised initially to set the charge. A charge set by a state agency will probably differ from a charge set by a federal agency. A charge set by a special board elected for the purpose will likely differ from a charge set by an existing pollution control agency. However, lacking a serviceable theory of how institutional differences between, say, the Congress and a regulatory agency shape the outcome of substantive policy, we must let the proponents of a charge scheme at the national, state, or local level weigh their chances and devise their tactics in the light of their more precise knowledge of the personalities and institutional peculiarities involved.

In a later section we compare the politics of charge-setting and charge enforcement with the politics of direct regulation and conclude that a charge system has some possible advantages for environmentalists. At this point we wish to emphasize the political

nature of the charge decision and to argue that this implies, normatively, a considerable role for a political rather than an administrative entity.

At the federal level, there are basically three different decision-making arrangements possible. First, a charge could be set by Congress, on the basis of information submitted by proponents and opponents; second, the charge-setting authority could be delegated to an agency; and third, the charge could be set by Congress, but with extensive interaction with agency staff and with a public review of alternatives.

Congress normally does not delegate "tax-setting" authority, but given the novel and ambiguous character of a "pollution charge," there might be less opposition to such a procedure than in the past. Perhaps a more precise formulation is that the tax committees have not delegated tax-setting authority, and if the taxation committees had jurisdiction it is much less likely that the charge setting would be delegated to an agency than if a pollution control committee had primary jurisdiction. In many other ways much would depend on whether the pollution control committees or the taxation committees had jurisdiction. The taxation committees have a strong claim to jurisdiction, but they have little expertise in environmental policy and are generally more responsive to business interests. On the other hand, the pollution control committees, particularly because of Senator Muskie, are more committed to the present direct regulation strategy than the taxation committees, though they are also probably more committed to effective environmental policies. Thus, even if the taxation committees approved the basic charge approach, they might be less than enthusiastic about high charge levels. Once a committee established jurisdiction, moreover, it would be difficult for another committee to amend the law. If the tax committees passed a pollution tax program but failed to institute an effectively high charge level, there might be little that the pollution control committees could do to increase the charge level (although they would have some bargaining influence because of their ability to reimpose or modify the direct regulation program). The most likely arrangement is some form of dual jurisdiction, although the jurisdictional question has not yet been settled: Senator Proxmire's water basin charge plan was referred to the pollution control commit-

tees; the Nixon administration's sulfur oxides charge proposal was sent to the House Ways and Means Committee.

Why might Congress not want to set the charge itself? Congressmen may not like to be forced to make the charge decision because its potential for economic disruption puts them on the spot politically, and forces them to make choices among competing and widely supported values. Congressmen may also feel they lack the technical information and competence to make such a complicated decision. On the other hand, the proponents of a charge may feel that their chances are better if Congress does not engage in extensive evaluation of the charge's justification and impacts, and instead may prefer the legislature to set broad constraints within which a more environmentally oriented agency can make the charge level decision.

In these circumstances, Congress could assign the charge-setting function to an existing or specially created agency. At the national level, the Environmental Protection Agency is the most likely candidate. The EPA's major advantage is its expertise on the costs and effectiveness of the abatement alternatives open to polluters. Its major disadvantages are that it cannot definitively weigh the social costs and benefits of its decision, and if it has the full charge-setting responsibility it may become, or seem to be, subject to political pressures that discredit its decision. While EPA has the best expertise on abatement costs of any federal agency, and given a year or two could develop much better data by industry sector, it may not want the responsibility for setting the charge. As one official concerned with this issue commented, EPA would prefer that Congress ultimately set the charge level because Congress can be more arbitrary than EPA. There is much to be said for this view. As our discussion of the information requirements of charge-setting showed, there are inevitably many tradeoffs among different values, judgments about how information deficiencies are to be treated, and which groups are to bear the burden of these uncertainties, that must be dealt with in any charge decision. An agency like EPA can certainly do the staff work and provide the information that Congress uses to decide the final charge level. But even if both Congress and the administrative agency use the same arbitrary rules of thumb in extrapolating from insufficient data, EPA must defend the inevitable arbitrariness on "technical"

grounds. Congress does not face these difficulties. It is constitutionally responsible for making value judgments for the nation. While the legislature must work within broad guidelines of justice and equity sanctioned by custom and law, it is normally engaged in weighing the costs to be borne by various groups and the significance to be given partial and incomplete data—the same kind of judgment that setting a charge involves.

Given the analytical deficiencies of a legislative committee, and the lack of political authority of a regulatory agency, the optimal charge-setting arrangement might be a cooperative or interactive process involving both. For charges, Congress could ask that EPA provide it with a set of different charge levels, and general charge arrangements, with the environmental and economic consequences of each option displayed. Congress could then choose whether to follow EPA's recommendations or, alternatively, accept another option. Charge levels and the performance of the system could be reviewed annually by the committees, with the data provided by the agency and other interested parties.

Alternatively, the obligation of Congress to decide a specific charge level could be obviated if regional charge-setting authorities were set up, in which case Congress might only mandate a minimum charge level and specify the procedures or criteria to be used in setting the charge. Still another alternative is to rely on a charge that automatically finds its effective level, in relation to the ambient standards of a regional airshed or river basin, rising by a certain amount each year that the ambient standards are not achieved and declining incrementally when they have been exceeded the previous year.

Revenue Addiction

One concern unique to the charge strategy is the fear that the charge will become mainly a revenue-raising device, with the charge set lower than is environmentally optimal in order to maximize revenue.[17] Adequate coverage of the major air and water pol-

---

[17] Theoretically, of course, there is a second revenue-maximization point: setting the charge much higher than needed for environmental purposes, with the firms being taxed exorbitantly before they can respond with abatement actions. Politically, however, this is not feasible.

lutants alone could generate several billions of dollars annually in the first years of operation if the charge were applied without a long grace period and aimed solely at reducing discharges. Even after polluters had several years to respond to the threat or actuality of the charge, the annual revenues could still be significant. But if the charge were set somewhat below the level at which polluters would be induced to abate, the annual revenue yield would be slightly less—but would continue almost indefinitely. This is the basis of the revenue-addiction fear that some key congressmen have voiced. They suspect that the financial temptation would produce strong pressures to emasculate the environmental effectiveness of the charge approach. Closely related to this, quite sensibly, is the question of where the charge revenue would go, of which interests would be vested by the charge revenue's continued flow. If the charge revenue went into the federal treasury, they suspect, the Treasury Department would have its own economic incentive to see to it that the revenue continued; this is similarly the case if all or part of the charge revenue were turned over to the states. On the other hand, if the charge revenue is earmarked for a particular purpose, presumably either environmental or compensatory, then all the disadvantages of a trust fund are possible. The public and private groups benefited by the trust fund will wish to see the funding continue. The risk is that the vested interests so created may become powerful enough to make it difficult to adjust the charge to the environmental optimum. Something of this sort may have happened in the offshore oil leasing program, for one writer notes that the desire to gain revenue for a conservation trust fund may have inhibited environmentalist objections to the oil drilling that eventually contaminated the Santa Barbara channel.[18]

If the continuation of the charge revenue is considered a serious problem, one possible solution is to tie the charge revenue to a program that has self-liquidating funding requirements. In this way the drying up of the charge revenue with the reduction in pollution dovetails nicely with the shrinkage in demand for its funds. One possible candidate for the self-liquidating program might be research and development on pollution abatement tech-

[18] Malcolm Baldwin and James K. Page, Jr., eds., *Law and the Environment* (New York, Walker, 1970).

niques. While there would undoubtedly be some dispute over which problems should be attended to, presumably as a particular industry reached high levels of abatement efficiency, there would be a decline in both the total charge revenue and the industry's demand for further research and development on its problems.

This discussion also demonstrates how interrelated the different features of a charge scheme are. With a charge plan that allows polluters an extended period of time before the charge is applied in full force, and that adjusts the charge automatically to the ambient standards, one need not worry; the revenue will be much less and those interested in revenue maximization will have no easy means of influencing the charge level.

Charge Systems at State and Local Levels

In general, the issues of initial implementation at the state level are analogous to those previously discussed for the national level. There are two issues, however, that are unique. The first concerns the problems facing the states that pioneer in pollution charges or other economic incentives to control environmental problems. The fear is that the first states to try charges might hurt their prospects for economic growth. If a state (or local) charge were high enough to be effective, firms might move out of the state, and new firms might hesitate to locate in the charge jurisdiction. This warning is usually as far as the analysis goes. A finer analysis must address the question of precisely which types of firms, realistically, have the motivation and option to move away or stay away, and which firms would be put out of business or be stunted in their growth because of the charge. Obviously, not all firms have serious waste problems or costly abatement alternatives. Still, many do. Within this class, there are great differences.

Electric power plants cannot easily move, though the cooperation of the state public utility commissions may be necessary so that the emission charge is not merely passed on as an added cost with no effort at abatement. (New York City has used SO_x charges on coal to give Consolidated Edison an incentive not to seek pollution standard variances from EPA, with apparent success.) Local services, such as laundries and meatpackers, which have a local market and are often sources of BOD, also cannot move easily. Natural resource-using firms, such as zinc, lead, or copper smelters,

owned by multiplant corporations, may or may not be able to relocate. In short, the state or local economy must be analyzed in detail before one knows how severely, if at all, it would be affected by a charge. Without such analysis, industry spokesmen will be able to claim that the charge will be catastrophic, or worse, and to recommend that charges be left to the national government (which they also know is presently disinclined to charges).

Some dislocation may be acceptable to a state or locality. After all, they realize that even under direct regulation there are some economic impacts. And like Vermont, which found that it gained clean industry when dirty firms left, the losses may not be unmatched even in economic terms. Finally, if the national effluent standards for new sources are effective, the high standards set for new plants may tend to make the states "noncompetitive" on new plants in the major industries, at least for pollution control costs.

The second difference between national and state charge systems concerns the additional alternatives for charge-setting mechanisms at the state level. At the state level there may be a greater inclination to try charge-setting arrangements not centered in the legislature or an existing state pollution control agency. Two possibilities are open. The first is a special charge setting board, either elected or appointed. By statute, such a board might be mandated to have a heavy representation of environmentalist and public members. In this way, the usual bias of such boards toward industry might be directly addressed and the board "tilted" toward more stringent environmental policies.

The second alternative charge-setting arrangement not available in national politics is the referendum. This was tried in Maine by environmental groups who felt impotent working through a legislature dominated by union and industry interests. In Maine the effluent charge proposal was consciously aimed at an effectively high "minimum" charge for important waterborne wastes, but it failed to gain enough signatures to be tested at the polls. In California, environmentalists have used the referendum strategy successfully in setting up the Coastal Zone Commission, but failed in their more ambitious Proposition Nine to set broad environmental policies for the state. The referendum strategy may be useful when state politicians are too beholden to industry (and union) interests and where there is reason to believe that the legislators' preferences do not accurately reflect those of their constituents.

Even if success is not likely, the referendum procedure may have an important educational function, popularizing the concept and forcing the issue onto the public agenda for debate. The referendum procedure has an unusual advantage over the normal electoral process. In any election campaign, voters choose candidates on the basis of many different qualities—their stands on various issues, personality, and party affiliation. A citizen interested in environmental issues will usually be interested in other issues as well; only rarely is there a single candidate who combines the right stand on all important issues with sterling personal qualities and the right party label. Thus when the proenvironment "bloc" goes to the polls, it often scatters its environmental sentiments among many other issues and personalities. A referendum is different. In a referendum on a pollution charge issue, the environmentalist bloc's influence is maximized because other distracting considerations are made irrelevant; the issue is only "for" or "against" tougher environmental policies and their consequences. This is no guarantee that the environmentalists will win on their issue, for the anti-environmental vote is also maximized. But it is an opportunity to determine the true sentiments of the voting population on these issues in a way that has immediate and direct political impact—something, for instance, that a public opinion poll cannot do.

In conclusion, with such opportunities and constraints, states can experiment with economic incentives intelligently and with relatively low risk. Oregon has had great success with its "bottle bill." New York City has apparently succeeded in making Consolidated Edison less eager to ask for variances to burn high sulfur coal with a newly imposed tax on SO_x. Vermont passed but later gutted a BOD charge system, and has had success with a land gains tax to control the environmental externalities of second home development. Many possibilities remain for applying charges to state and local environmental problems.

The Politics of an Operating Charge System

The previous discussion has focused almost exclusively on the politics of enacting and initially implementing a pollution charge

system—the major actors and the issues they see as important, and the design tradeoffs that have special political significance. Important as these questions are to a country which has not had any experience with the practical political and administrative problems of a pollution charge system, a different set of political issues must also be addressed: Are the political assets and liabilities of a charge system—once in place—likely to be superior, on balance, to those of the present effluent standards system?

By political assets and liabilities we mean such important considerations as whether the enforcement process under effluent standards is likely to be as susceptible to delay and informal bargaining pressures from polluters as the present system, and whether the actual level of the charge is likely to be high enough to be effective.

Naturally, answers to these questions depend on the specific enforcement procedures chosen and the specific institutional arrangements for setting the charge level. Nonetheless, general comparisons can be made between charges and direct regulation.

The Politics of Enforcement

Under direct regulation, the pollution control agency determines what discharge reductions a polluter must achieve by a certain date, and then the law-abiding polluter installs the required abatement equipment. For those few who fail to meet the standards on time, variances must be obtained from the agency after justifying the slippage in cleanup performance, or else the waste discharger will find himself in court facing a fine for his violations. Such is the theory.

In practice, the process is a Rube Goldberg delight, laden with political vulnerabilities and administrative difficulties that defeat even the best-intentioned administrators. A direct regulation system has two inherent defects: First, it cannot obtain the information it needs to set effluent standards that will stand up politically and judicially. Second, polluters have such powerful incentives to delay complying that the enforcement resources of the agency are overwhelmed, and the enforcement authority and manpower needed to compensate for these perverse incentives are so enor-

mous that the regulatory agency will never obtain them in a political system influenced by strong business interests.

We can be fairly confident that a properly designed charge system is much less susceptible to corruption and ineffectiveness in
administration than a system of direct regulation. It is this way
because the information it requires for enforcement is changed
from hard-to-obtain technical-economic feasibility data to easily
obtained emission monitor readings, and because the charge encourages polluters to minimize their costs by finding ways of reducing their emissions rather than by stymieing the environmental
control agency. These qualities make the charge system, potentially, an administrative automaton, with relatively little vulner-
ability to administrative ineffectiveness and corruption. This very
quality, however, makes the system critically dependent on the
precise level of the charge. What, then, are the chances that environmental proponents of a charge would fare any better in per-
suading Congress to pass an effective pollution control program
than they have in the past?

The Politics of Setting the Charge

The question of setting the charge concerns mainly the political
advantages and disadvantages of a charge program in the legislative arena. Our thesis is that the information necessary to draw up
a charge schedule may give the charge system many practical political advantages over the present arrangements. These advantages
derive from its enhanced potential for greater publicness and the
centralization of analysis and decision making.

PUBLICNESS AND CENTRALIZATION.   While a national charge system would centralize analysis and decision making, the greater
publicness of the charge-setting process is a potential that may or
may not be realized in practice. Thus, if charge-setting were centered in the Congress, as it began to consider a charge schedule,
good information would tend to call forth better information.
The predictions of government economists would certainly be dis-
puted or given further backing by the affected parties, industry,
and environmental groups. Industry data would be criticized and
firms challenged to supply more detailed information. Already, for

example, the fear of an effluent charge program has led one large paper and pulp manufacturer to offer to let EPA audit its books so the EPA can see how disastrous, in the firm's opinion, the charge would be. Such precedents, and the cost-of-abatement data that are gathered under the various permit programs and through government-sponsored studies of industry sectors would make cost and performance data more accessible to the public. Nonindustry engineers and economists would be able to analyze the data and assumptions of the government and industry studies. Out of the ensuing debate, better calculations of the consequences and of ways to minimize adverse effects could emerge.

In effect, the numerous public hearings mandated at the local, state, and federal levels would be combined into one high-level public forum, either in congressional committee hearings or public hearings called by EPA. The very criticality of the decision—deriving from the centralization of decision making and the known importance of the charge schedule to the whole program—would give these hearings and the accompanying political debate a salience that would otherwise be lacking in a standards program in which there would be a multitude of important parameters and whose control would be dispersed throughout many different political and bureaucratic jurisdictions. With such salience, the political decision might be more likely to favor effectively high charges or, depending on the evaluation of public sentiments (and the representatives of Congress in expressing those sentiments), a balance would be struck between environmental and nonenvironmental values that accurately reflect the price this society is willing to pay for the proffered environmental benefits.

This is, potentially, a remarkable departure from the present process of deciding on and implementing environmental policy. It is not so much that charge-setting requires different kinds of information as that it uses the information in a very different way. Both direct regulation and charge systems need information on the cost and effectiveness of different abatement options, and on the discharges of polluters. In both systems, the monitoring need be only as accurate as necessary to ensure consistent compliance. As chapter 4 shows, this depends on the predictability of the variation in emissions of the polluter. If, for example, emissions do not vary, then the firm need only be monitored once; on the other

hand, if emissions vary from hour to hour and are not predictable by accurate formulas relating emissions to other more easily determined production values (such as pounds of fuel used), then monitoring might have to be hourly. But this is true for both systems.

On the other hand, charge systems can use *aggregate* abatement cost-effectiveness information where direct regulation often needs more accurate and particularized information at either the standard-setting or standard-enforcing stage. Now, it might be objected that this is merely an argument for the centralization of decision making and analysis, rather than for the unique advantages of a charge system, and that a uniform national system of direct regulation would have the same advantages. This is not the case, however, because of an important consequence of using aggregate data—the asymmetry in the way that abatement cost and effectiveness data are used in the two systems. *Charge setting depends less than direct regulation on finely accurate abatement performance information because the consequences of being somewhat inaccurate are not as severe for the polluter or the pollution control agency.* Charges, unlike direct regulation, give firms the option of paying the charge; in theory, the polluter does not have to face serious penalties if the effluent standards are not attained, and thus the abatement information does not have to be accurate enough to convince a judge that the firm is not being asked to do something impossible. This means that the charge can be based partly on future expectations of performance possibilities rather than only on what is practicable or proven today. This leeway in possible "error" allows charges to be uniform where agencies administering standards are under heavy political and judicial pressure to consider all important differences in initial situations and immediate prospects. The different ways that the two systems can treat abatement performance information produces results favorable to environmentalists. One effect is that the major advantage of industry—its indisputable expertise in knowing the fine distinctions between different firms and the technical complexities of different production technologies and abatement techniques—is devalued. Although highly accurate information is always desirable, only major differences and orders of magnitude in costs and performance are critical, and with these data outside economists can construct the sophisticated linear programming economic response

models for each industry that will tell what the gross economic impacts are likely to be and the emission diffusion models that predict what charge level will achieve the desired ambient standards.[19]

The use of aggregate cost effectiveness data in a centralized and open decision making forum has an extremely important institutional consequence. It means that the resources of the opposing sides are likely to be more equalized, with environmental groups having a relatively greater influence on the final decision than they would have on the effluent standard decisions made by a multitude of jurisdictions. Instead of having to fight in many different places—with much less likelihood that the outcome would have much effect on actual behavior—a single centralized and highly salient decision-making forum would make it worthwhile for non-industry engineers and economists to spend their time scrutinizing the data and assumptions behind government and industry charge calculations and to participate in this analytically sophisticated political process. Such a change favors groups with fewer numbers and monetary resources but with competitive analytical skills, a characteristic of the environmental and academic proponents of the charge approach.

ECONOMICS-ORIENTED DEBATES.   One possible disadvantage of a charge-setting situation is that the public debate may be infused with economic assumptions and thus may tend to consider the costs of pollution control more heavily than the costs of pollution. This may be exacerbated by the possibility that the debate over charges will take place in a political climate not as favorable to environmental goals as the early 1970s. In fact, the opportunity for a charge plan to get on the public agenda may result mainly from a complete reevaluation of environmental goals as well as means.

[19] Of course, one *can* design a charge system that needs abatement cost-effectiveness information as accurate and specific as the most demanding system of direct regulation by making the charge custom-fitted to each firm's particular situation—but this would be foolish. (See Delogu, "A State Approach to Effluent Charges," for an example of just such a charge system.) The charge systems we recommend here are uniform over a large set of firms, either region- or industrywide. Naturally, the smaller the geographical area or number of firms in an area, for example, the less likely the differences in estimation errors are to average out, and the more accurate the abatement information may have to be to satisfy opponents and proponents that it is neither an overcharge nor an undercharge.

Environmental goals are not as widely perceived "motherhood" issues as they were in Earth Day times. Today it is more apparent that achieving environmental goals often involves costly tradeoffs of other widely held values. This may explain a puzzle: While there is no significant difference between the economic dislocation produced by strictly enforced effluent standards under direct regulation and that produced by an equivalent charge system (in fact, direct regulation has higher overall and average costs), talk of imposing a pollution charge seems to bring out a discussion, almost from the start, of the economic impacts of pollution control. Here we must look to the nature of the agreement supposedly reached on environmental policy.

In the welfare economics textbooks, an environmental goal would be decided upon by comparing the environmental costs and benefits with the nonenvironmental costs and benefits. In the American experience, however, national environmental ambient standards generally have not been arrived at by this balancing process; they have been defined by considering mainly the social costs of pollution, with Congress specifying, for example, that the ambient air quality was to be at a level that precluded *any* discernible adverse effects on health; the exact figures for the standards were to be filled in by technicians and the goals achieved by arbitrarily determined deadlines. This means that the costs of achieving these goals are enormous, and perhaps intolerable in terms of other goals, if strictly construed. Since the costs of abatement do matter to politicians, the result is that the cost is controlled by making the enforcement process weak and slippery, insinuating elastic technical-economic feasibility criteria into the effluent standards, and setting long-range deadlines for the achievement of grandiose goals.

Charges, on the other hand, naively take these grand goals as true goals, and proceed to impose a much more effective enforcement mechanism for achieving them. Because charges provide such an extremely strong incentive for polluters to abate, charges thus take a basically infeasible long-term goal whose achievement was realistically calculated as decades away and transform it into a goal that can be realized much more quickly. As such they inevitably bring to the fore previously buried issues about costs and benefits, and in a way that is hard to sidestep.

There are two likely consequences for the politics of a charge system. First, the proponents of a charge plan will be asked to predict the economic effects of their charge with an accuracy never required of the present system of direct regulation. Second, there are likely to be heavy adaptive burdens placed on a charge plan to make it fit in with the preexisting control program. This is because by the time a charge plan is considered, many firms will have invested in equipment designed to meet the old standards set by regulatory agencies, and a charge plan is likely to be required that won't penalize firms that have in good faith adapted to the old system. Custom-fitting in such a complex situation will place a greater burden on a charge plan, and may in the end overtax the analytical capabilities of the charge's proponents. This depends, of course, on the time and resources available for designing a charge plan; and the problem will be most acute if the opportunity to reconsider environmental policy and consider a charge substitute or supplement arrives and "peaks" in a short period of time, leaving charge proponents with a short lead time in which to prepare their arguments.

Conclusion

The foregoing potential disadvantages of charges seem to boil down to a restatement of the need for a charge plan to be well designed, to be designed to be politically feasible in the particular context involved. Overall, charges seem to have enough potential advantages over other alternatives at the legislative level to justify their implementation. They will be opposed by industrialists out of self-interest; probably by regulatory authorities out of fear of the consequences of admitting that the present policies have failed, and from misunderstandings grounded in the engineering and legal outlooks of regulatory personnel; and by those politicians who stand to lose by the change to a different and more publicly visible pollution control strategy. But if a new policy had to wait until there was no opposition, nothing would ever be changed. Pollution charges, potentially at least, have such great administrative and economic efficiency, and even equity advantages over the existing approach that they are worth pursuing seriously in the political arena.

Index

Library of Congress Cataloging in Publication Data

Main entry under title:

Environmental improvement through economic incentives.

1. Environmental policy. 2. Pollution—Costs.
3. Pollution—Economic aspects. I. Anderson,
Frederick R. II. Resources for the Future.
HC79.E5E578   301.31   76-47400
ISBN 0-8018-2000-6
ISBN 0-8018-2100-2 pbk.